SpringerBriefs in Education

We are delighted to announce SpringerBriefs in Education, an innovative product type that combines elements of both journals and books. Briefs present concise summaries of cutting-edge research and practical applications in education. Featuring compact volumes of 50 to 125 pages, the SpringerBriefs in Education allow authors to present their ideas and readers to absorb them with a minimal time investment. Briefs are published as part of Springer's eBook Collection. In addition, Briefs are available for individual print and electronic purchase.

SpringerBriefs in Education cover a broad range of educational fields such as: Science Education, Higher Education, Educational Psychology, Assessment & Evaluation, Language Education, Mathematics Education, Educational Technology, Medical Education and Educational Policy.

SpringerBriefs typically offer an outlet for:

- An introduction to a (sub)field in education summarizing and giving an overview of theories, issues, core concepts and/or key literature in a particular field
- A timely report of state-of-the art analytical techniques and instruments in the field of educational research
- A presentation of core educational concepts
- An overview of a testing and evaluation method
- A snapshot of a hot or emerging topic or policy change
- An in-depth case study
- A literature review
- A report/review study of a survey
- An elaborated thesis

Both solicited and unsolicited manuscripts are considered for publication in the SpringerBriefs in Education series. Potential authors are warmly invited to complete and submit the Briefs Author Proposal form. All projects will be submitted to editorial review by editorial advisors.

SpringerBriefs are characterized by expedited production schedules with the aim for publication 8 to 12 weeks after acceptance and fast, global electronic dissemination through our online platform SpringerLink. The standard concise author contracts guarantee that:

- an individual ISBN is assigned to each manuscript
- each manuscript is copyrighted in the name of the author
- the author retains the right to post the pre-publication version on his/her website or that of his/her institution

Lucas Kohnke

Using Technology to Design ESL/EFL Microlearning Activities

 Springer

Lucas Kohnke
Department of English Language Education
The Education University of Hong Kong
Hong Kong, China

ISSN 2211-1921   ISSN 2211-193X (electronic)
SpringerBriefs in Education
ISBN 978-981-99-2773-9   ISBN 978-981-99-2774-6 (eBook)
https://doi.org/10.1007/978-981-99-2774-6

This Springer imprint is published by the registered company Springer Nature Singapore Pte Ltd.
The registered company address is: 152 Beach Road, #21-01/04 Gateway East, Singapore 189721, Singapore

*To my wife Jannifer and my son Oskar
without whom this book would been
completed one year earlier.*

Preamble

Although there is a growing body of knowledge on technology-enhanced language learning, at the time I decided to write this book, I could not find any published books addressing the design of English as a Second Language (ESL) and English as a Foreign Language (EFL) microlearning activities. I have taught technology courses for pre-and in-service English teachers at the Education University of Hong Kong, focusing on developing microlearning activities ('Integrating ICT in the ESL classroom'; 'Effective use of e-resources in primary/secondary English classrooms'; 'Sustainable development of e-learning in schools') and delivered workshops on this topic around the world. However, I have realized it is difficult to find relevant literature that explains microlearning, the use of technology, and the design of ESL/ EFL activities. Moreover, my students have repeatedly asked for such a resource, showing the urgent need for this book.

Due to the COVID-19 pandemic, students have been unable to attend face-to-face classes and have been forced to engage in online learning (Moorhouse & Kohnke, 2021a). In the post-pandemic world, teachers need resources to effectively deal with the 'new normal' of education and integrate technology into their ESL/EFL lessons (Moorhouse & Kohnke, 2021b). Microlearning is critical for teachers who want to maximize their students' learning by using bite-sized chunks of content that can be completed anytime and anywhere (Kohnke & Foung, in-press).

This book is intended to serve as a practical resource for language teachers. Thus, its goals are twofold: (1) to shed light on microlearning as a rapidly emerging phenomenon in ESL/EFL teaching and learning and (2) to provide strategies, tools, and best practices for incorporating microlearning in English lessons, including activities that teachers can modify to their contexts based on their learners' language proficiency, needs, and interests. In doing so, it aims to help teachers create and deliver microlearning activities that are optimized for mobile learning and ESL/EFL students. The book draws on the relevant literature and my first-hand experience developing microlearning activities. It is a useful starting point for language teachers who are interested in the principles of designing microlearning activities for the ESL/EFL classroom.

Hong Kong, China   Lucas Kohnke

Acknowledgements The success of a project hinges on the dedication, commitment, and generosity of various organizations and individuals. Without their unwavering support and eagerness to foster a collaborative environment, this project would not have been such a rewarding experience. Therefore, I extend my heartfelt appreciation to the following people who made this book possible:

- My colleagues in the Department of English Language Education, The Education University of Hong Kong
- My loving wife and son

References

Kohnke, L. & Foung, D. (2013). Exploring microlearning for CALL teacher education and professional development: Voices from Hong Kong. In D. Tafazoli & M. Picard (Eds.), *CALL teacher education and professional development: Voices from under-represented context* (pp. 279–292). Cham: Springer. https://doi.org/10.1007/978-981-99-0514-0_17

Moorhouse, B. L., & Kohnke, L. (2021a). Thriving or surviving emergency remote teaching necessitated by COVID-19: University teachers' perspectives. *The Asia-Pacific Education Researcher*, *30*, 279–287. https://doi.org/10.1007/s40299-021-00567-9

Moorhouse, B. L., & Kohnke, L. (2021b). Responses of the english language-teaching community to the COVID-19 pandemic. *RELC J.*, *52*(3), 359–378. https://doi.org/10.1177%2F0033688221 1053052

Contents

Chapter 1
Microlearning as a Teaching and Learning Approach

Abstract This chapter begins with an introduction to the concept of microlearning, providing a thorough definition and discussing its key characteristics. The role of microlearning as a teaching and learning approach will then be examined, as will its potential benefits and applications in ESL/EFL contexts. We will then present the rationale for writing this book, outlining the primary goals and intended audience. Finally, a synopsis of the book's content will be presented.

Keywords Microlearning · ESL · EFL · Technology · Mobile devices · Mobile learning

1.1 What is Microlearning?

Conventional learning can be dull, difficult, and time-consuming. Learners are no longer interested in watching or listening to a full, traditional lecture. Instead, they are inclined to use mobile applications to learn English (Godwin-Jones, 2011; Kohnke, 2020; Kohnke & Ting, 2021; Kohnke et al., 2021), which has spurred interest in the pedagogical potential of such applications (Goggins et al., 2013). Learners can use them to acquire knowledge precisely when they need it or experience curiosity. It has long been recognized that using technology to provide appropriate and timely content can be a catalyst for language learning (Li, 2017). Recent changes to the educational and technological landscape have prompted educators to provide bite-sized chunks of input—an approach called microlearning.

The role of technology in English as a second language (ESL) and English as a foreign language (EFL) education has changed dramatically since the outbreak of the COVID-19 pandemic in early 2020 (Moorhouse & Kohnke, 2021). Conventional learning is no longer preferred by students and teachers. Classes are now taught in various modalities, including in-person, online, and hybrid. Therefore, ESL/EFL teachers must consider new approaches to their lessons. While the situation continues to evolve and take different forms, microlearning has nevertheless become a significant topic in the field of language education.

Microlearning has been around for decades (Hug et al., 2005) but experienced a resurgence when face-to-face classes were suspended and students had to learn from home during the pandemic (Kohnke et al., in-press). This situation forced ESL/EFL teachers to create trimodal (in-person, synchronous online, asynchronous online) learning environments and ensure that they remained student-centred (Adedoyin & Soykan, 2020; Kohnke & Moorhouse, 2022). This phenomenon continues to drive curriculum design and pedagogy in the post-COVID-19 learning environment.

Microlearning comprises a blend of various delivery methods leveraging the most effective components of each. As such, it puts the learner at the centre of the educational experience, embraces multi-sensory/multi-modal design, and uses technological tools to increase student engagement and achievement (Dolasinski & Reynolds, 2019). Because it integrates a multisensory/multimodal design, microlearning is more likely to resonate with individual students, impact teaching and learning positively, and increase students' knowledge retention and satisfaction.

1.2   Definition

Despite the widespread interest in the topic, the term microlearning has not been adequately defined to date. Maddox (2018) defined it as 'an approach to learning that conveys information about a single, specific idea in a compact and focused manner' (p. 1), but did not specify what constitutes 'compact and focused'. Accordingly, there is agreement that microlearning activities should be short, but not *how* short—nor how they can best be delivered. For example, Hug et al. (2005) proposed that a microlearning activity can last 'less than a second up to more than one hour' (p. 3) On the other hand, Torgerson (2016) argued that microlearning content must be consumed within 5 min. Shank (2018) stated that 'microlearning must be primarily about learning, not content' (para. 11) and 'not mostly about technology' (para. 12), whereas Hug et al. (2005) suggested it could be delivered either face-to-face or using technology.

The changes in the learning environment due to the COVID-19 pandemic made mobile microlearning an effective, accessible, personalized learning format that engaged learners who could not access physical classrooms. Today, learners are used to bite-sized chunks that are less overwhelming than traditional methods, personalized learning experiences that allow them to work at their own pace and revisit topics as needed, and interactive elements such as videos, quizzes, and podcasts.

This book defines a microlearning activity as a 2–8 min activity that effectively provides focused, personalized content using technology. It should be 'snackable'—a concise 'nugget' optimized for mobile learning (Jahnke et al., 2020). Moreover, it considers how microlearning addresses the needs of various ESL/EFL learners, including early childhood, primary, secondary, tertiary, and adult learners.

1.3 Microlearning as a Teaching and Learning Approach

Various studies indicate that microlearning is a promising approach to teaching and learning across disciplines (e.g. language, engineering, nursing; Fang, 2018; Hui, 2014; Zheng et al., 2019). This is because it encourages the use of different delivery methods to help learners focus on the key information and mitigate the impact of diminishing attention spans. However, adopting microlearning requires language teachers to rethink traditional methods of delivering course content. It embraces learning formats such as PDFs, podcasts, infographics, videos, augmented reality, and chatbots, which prioritize essential messages or bursts of information (Kohnke, 2021). Each 'chunk' focuses on a single idea (e.g. a specific grammar point) to reduce the risk of cognitive overload (Epp and Phirangee, 2019; Nikou, 2019) and promote better retention (Jomah et al., 2016).

For example, a teacher could deliver a short video lecture and then ask students to complete a follow-up activity based on the video. Previous studies have found that short videos can be effective methods of delivering content both in and outside of classroom settings (Tiernan & O'Kelly, 2019). There is also a correlation between video views and student satisfaction (Beatty et al., 2019). Follow-up activities could integrate visuals and infographics to remind learners of the content and encourage both short- and long-term retention (Rajagopal et al., 2019; VanderMolen & Spivey, 2017). Another example of a follow-up activity is a writing (e.g. Google Docs) or speaking (e.g. Flipgrid) task in which students organize and demonstrate their learning.

As learners can access microlearning activities, such as streaming videos and gamified activities, using their mobile devices (Kohnke, 2021), they promote self-regulation and lifelong learning (Reinhard & Elwood, 2019). They also allow learners to interact and connect with each other and the content anytime and anywhere (Torgerson & Lannone, 2019). Moreover, teachers can remove content that could distract students to create a concise and focused experience. Microlearning can also provide learners with small achievement milestones that further motivate them and increase their engagement (Shamir-Inbal & Blau, 2022). The approach centres learners, as activities can be adapted based on their preferences (Davis & Arend, 2013), which facilitates self-directed learning (Bell, 2010; Cosneyfroy & Carre, 2014) and increases knowledge (Gagne et al., 2019; Wang et al., 2020). In addition, it caters to the preferences of students who have been digitally connected since childhood (Reinhardt & Elwood, 2019) and are accustomed to mobile devices, social media, and the quick burst of information that comes from a simple Google search.

Technology integration is the 'new normal' in education. Microlearning offers a new way to engage students and deliver student-centred learning.

1.4 Book Overview

This book is divided into chapters. The second chapter offers an overview of technological trends in language education. Chapter 3 delves into the pedagogical principles of designing microlearning activities for the ESL/EFL classroom, as well as the complex issues arising from the experience. The fourth chapter investigates how mobile microlearning can improve listening, speaking, writing, and reading skill. In Chap. 5, readers will learn how to create microlearning activities with podcasts, videos, infographics, and flashcards. The sixth chapter focuses on creating microlearning activities with virtual and augmented reality. Chatbots are introduced in Chap. 7, along with how they can be used in accordance with microlearning principles. Finally, future possibilities for microlearning in education are discussed in Chap. 8.

This book is a concise but comprehensive introduction to the field, which draws on relevant literature and the author's first-hand experience. It serves as an important starting point for teachers, curriculum developers, academics, and scholars interested in the principles and practices of microlearning in the ESL/EFL classroom.

References

Adedoyin, O. B., & Soykan, E. (2020). Covid-19 pandemic and online learning: The challenges and opportunities. *Interactive Learning Environments*. https://doi.org/10.1080/10494820.2020.1813180

Beatty, B. J., Merchant, Z., & Albert, M. (2019). Analysis of student use of video in a flipped classroom. *Tech Trends, 63*(4), 376–385. https://doi.org/10.1007/s11528-017-0169-1

Bell, F. (2010). Network theories for technology-enabled learning and social change: Connectivism and actor network theory. In *Proceedings of Networked Learning Conference: Seventh International Conference on Networked Learning Aalborg/Denmark*. Digital collection of University of Salford.

Cosnefroy, L., & Carré, P. (2014). Self-regulated and self-directed learning: Why don't some neighbors communicate? *International Journal Self-Directed Learning, 11*(2), 1–12.

Davis, J. R., & Arend, B. (2013). *Seven ways of learning: A resource for more purposeful, effective, and enjoyable college teaching*. Stylus Publishing.

Dolasinski, M. J., & Reynolds, J. (2019). Microlearning in the higher education hospitality classroom. *Journal of Hospitality & Tourism Education*. https://doi.org/10.1080/10963758.2021.1963748

Epp, C. D., & Phirangee, K. (2019). Exploring mobile tool integration: Design activities carefully or students may not learn. *Contemporary Educational Psychology, 59*. https://doi.org/10.1016/j.cedpsych.2019.101791

Fang, Q. (2018). A study of college English teaching mode in the context of micro-learning. In *International Conference on Management and Education, Humanities and Social Sciences (MEHSS 2018)*. Atlantis Press.

Gagne, J. C., Park, K. H., Hall, K., Woodward, A., Yamane, S., & Kim, S. S. (2019). Microlearning in health professions education: Scoping review. *JMIR Medical Education, 5*(2). Retrieved from https://mededu.jmir.org/2019/2/e13997/

Godwin-Jones, R. (2011). Mobile apps for language learning. *Language Learning & Technology, 15*, 2–11.

Goggins, S. P., Jahnke, I., & Wulf, V. (2013). *Computer-supported collaborative learning at the workplace.* Springer.

Hug, T., Lindner, M., & Bruck, P. (2005). *Microlearning: Emerging concepts, practices and technologies after e-learning.* Innsbruck University Press.

Hui, B. (2014). Application of micro-learning in physiology teaching for adult nursing specialty students. *Journal of Qiqihar University of Medicine, 21*(61). Retrieved October 16, 2022, from http://en.cnki.com.cn/Article_en/CJFDTOTAL-QQHB201421061.htm

Jahnke, I., Lee, Y.-M., Pham, M., He, H., & Austin, L. (2020). Unpacking the inherent design principles of mobile microlearning. *Technology, Knowledge, and Learning, 25,* 585–619. https://doi.org/10.1007/s10758-019-09413-w

Jomah, O., Masoud, A. K., Kishore, X. P., & Sagaya, A. (2016). Micro learning: A modernized education system. *Broad Research in Artificial Intelligence and Neroscience,* 103–110.

Kohnke, L. (2020). Exploring learner perception, experience and motivation of using a mobile app in L2 vocabulary acquisition. *International Journal of Computer-Assisted Language Learning and Teaching, 10*(1), 15–26. https://doi.org/10.4018/IJCALLT.2020010102

Kohnke, L. (2021). Optimizing microlearning for mobile learning. In J. R. Corbeil, M. E. Corbeil, & B. H. Khan (Eds.), *Microlearning in the digital age: The design and delivery of learning in snippets* (pp. 80–94). Routledge.

Kohnke, L., Foung, D., & Zou, D. (in-press). Microlearning: A new normal for flexible teacher professional development in online and blended learning. *Education and Information Technologies.*

Kohnke, L., & Moorhouse, B. (2022). Facilitating synchronous online language learning through Zoom. *RELC Journal, 53*(1), 261–265. https://doi.org/10.1177/0033688220937235

Kohnke, L., & Ting, A. (2021). ESL students' perceptions of mobile applications for discipline-specific vocabulary acquisition for academic purposes. *Knowledge Management & E-Learning, 13*(1), 102–117. https://doi.org/10.34105/j.kmel.2021.13.006

Kohnke, L., Zou, D., & Zhang, R. (2021). Exploring discipline-specific vocabulary retention in L2 through app design: Implications for higher education students. *RELC Journal, 52*(3), 539–556. https://doi.org/10.1177/0033688219899740

Li, L. (2017). *New technologies and language learning.* Palgrave: London, UK.

Maddox, T. (2018). Microlearning and the brain. Retrieved from Chief Learning Officer: https://www.chieflearningofficer.com/article-author/toddmaddox/

Moorhouse, B. L., &. Kohnke, L. (2021). Responses of the English-language teaching community to the COVID-19 Pandemic. *RELC Journal, 52*(3), 359–378. https://doi.org/10.1177/003368 82211053052

Nikou, S. (2019). A micro-learning based model to enhance student teachers' motivation and engagement in blended learning. In K. Graziano (Ed.), *Proceedings of Society for Information Technology & Teacher Education International Conference* (pp. 509–514). Association for the Advancement of Computing in Education (AACE).

Rajagopal, L., Reynolds, J., & Li, D. (2019). Visual-based minimal-text food safety training materials for Chinese-speaking foodservice workers. *Journal of Extension, 57*(5). Retrieved from https://tigerprints.clemson.edu/joe/vol57/iss5/25

Reinhardt, K. S., & Elwood, S. (2019). Promising practices in online training and support: Microlearning and personal learning environments to promote a growth mindset in learners. In J. Keengwe (Ed.), *Handbook of research on virtual training and mentoring of online instructors* (pp. 298–310). IGI Global.

Shamir-Inbal, T. & Blau, I. (2022). Micro-learning in designing professional development for ICT teacher leaders: The role of self-regulation and perceived learning. *Professional Development in Education, 48*(5), 734-750.https://doi.org/10.1080/19415257.2020.1763434

Shank, P. (2018). Microlearning, macrolearning. What does research tell us? *eLearning Industry.* Retrieved on February 20, 2023 from https://elearningindustry.com/microlearning-macrolearning-research-tell-us

Tiernan, P., & O'Kelly, J. (2019). Learning with digital video in second level schools in Ireland. *Education and Information Technologies, 24*(2), 1073–1088. https://doi.org/10.1007/s10639-018-9811-6

Torgerson, C. (2016). *The microlearning guide to microlearning*. Torgeson Consulting.

VanderMolen, J., & Spivey, C. (2017). Creating infographics to enhance student engagement and communication in health economics. *The Journal of Economic Education, 48*(3), 198–205. https://doi.org/10.1080/00220485.2017.1320605

Wang, C., Bakhet, M., Roberts, D., Gnani, S., & El-Osta, A. (2020). The efficacy of microlearning in improving self-care capability: A systematic review of the literature. *Public Health, 186*, 286–296. https://doi.org/10.1016/j.puhe.2020.07.007

Zheng, R., Zhu, J., Zhang, M., Liu, R., Wu, Q., & Yang, L. (2019). A novel resource deployment approach to mobile micro- learning: From energy-saving perspective. *Wireless Communications and Mobile Computing*, 1–15. https://doi.org/10.1155/2019/7430860

Chapter 2
Overview of Technology in Teaching and Learning

Abstract This chapter provides an overview of the use of technology in teaching and learning from the 1970s to the present to help the reader understand the theory and practice of mobile microlearning. The chapter has three themes: an overview of Computer-assisted language learning based pedagogy, an introduction to mobile-assisted language learning, and an introduction to theories of learning.

Keywords Computer-assisted language learning · Mobile-assisted language learning · CALL · MALL

2.1 Computer-Assisted Language Learning (CALL)

In the late 1960s, technology was integrated into second- and foreign-language education through the use of large mainframe computers that offered learners repetitive language drills (i.e. drill-and-practice method). Since then, the pedagogical benefits of technology have increased due to the constant evolution of hardware, software, and internet connectivity, as well as the introduction of micro-computers into schools in the early 1980s. It has shifted from using simple audiovisual tools (e.g. cassettes, CDs, videos) to enhance learners' listening comprehension to presenting rich, interactive learning content on laptops, tablets, and smartphones using student response systems (e.g. Mentimeter, Kahoot, GoSoapBox, Poll Everywhere) and student engagement platforms (e.g. Nearpod, EdApp) (see Kohnke & Moorhouse, 2021; Kohnke, 2021; Moorhouse & Kohnke, 2020). Therefore, technology use is an essential part of the modern language classroom.

Since the 1960s, many different terms have been used to describe the development of computer-assisted language learning (CALL) (e.g. Chapelle, 2001; Chun, 2016, 2019; Levy, 2000; Warschauer, 2004). Table 2.1 presents the four main theoretical movements in the history of CALL teaching.

The first phase, structural CALL, dates back to the 1970s and was influenced by grammar-translation and audio-lingual methods. Teachers used mainframe technology in language learning labs to enhance students' accuracy through the 'drill-and-practice' technique. Learners were expected to learn the language and its rules

© The Author(s), under exclusive license to Springer Nature Singapore Pte Ltd. 2023
L. Kohnke, *Using Technology to Design ESL/EFL Microlearning Activities*,
SpringerBriefs in Education, https://doi.org/10.1007/978-981-99-2774-6_2

Table 2.1 Stages of CALL

Stage	1970s–1980s: structural CALL	1980s–1990s: communicative CALL	2000s: integrative CALL	2010s: ecological CALL
Technology	Mainframe	PCs	Multimedia and internet	Mobile and wearable devices
Language teaching paradigm	Grammar-translation and audio-lingual	Communicative language teaching	CLIL, ESP/EAP	Digital literacies, multi-literacies
View of language	Structural (a formal structural system)	Cognitive (a mentally constructed system)	Socio-cognitive (developed in social interaction)	Sociocultural (interactional competence and intercultural competence)
Principal use of computers	Drill and practice	Communicative exercises	Authentic discourse	Global communication and knowledge co-construction
Principal objective	Accuracy	Accuracy and fluency	Accuracy, fluency, and agency	Identity as global citizens
Principal role of computers	Provide drill, practice, tutorial explanations, and corrective feedback	Provide language input and analytic or influential tasks	Provide alternative contexts for social interaction	Provide a space/environment for people to communicate and construct knowledge

Chun (2019, p. 1), Li (2017, p. 14)

by constant imitation and mechanical drills. Language learning was broken down into sequential steps, each covering a piece of the subject domain or a particular skill.

The second phase of CALL, based on the communicative language teaching paradigm, emerged around 1980 and lasted through the 1990s. Teachers used personal computers to expose learners to language in context and facilitate acquisition. Unlike structural CALL, communicative CALL allowed learners to control the learning process, pace, and content. Research focused on the effective use of language learning labs, and additional CALL materials were introduced, including courseware and CD-ROMs for self-study.

As the internet became accessible and more multimedia content became available in the 2000s, the third phase (integrative CALL) emerged. There were few limitations regarding where and when learning could take place. In addition, teachers began using authentic online resources to provide more agency to learners taking English for Specific Purposes (ESP), English for Academic Purposes (EAP), and Content and Language Integrated Learning (CLIL) courses.

From 2010 onwards, ecological CALL (the fourth stage) has allowed learners to acquire language through ubiquitous technologies, such as mobile/wearable devices that connect to the internet. Teachers focus on allowing learners to communicate globally and enhance their digital literacies. Mobile-assisted language learning (MALL) has also become increasingly common, enabling students to learn anytime and anywhere (Kohnke, 2020).

2.2   Mobile-Assisted Language Learning (MALL)

Mobile technologies play a vital part in our daily lives (Liu & Chen, 2015) and have been available for more than two decades (Burston, 2014a). MALL is different from CALL because it focuses on the use of personal, portable devices—initially, MP3/MP4 players (e.g. iPods), personal digital assistants, and palmtop computers. Over the past decade, educators have begun to understand how to usefully deploy MALL for language acquisition (Morgana & Kukulska-Hulme, 2021). Like early CALL, the first MALL programs followed a transmission model approach to "support teacher-learner communication and use the mobile device to deliver content" (Kukulska-Hulme & Shield, 2008, p. 274). As a result, MALL has traditionally been teacher-centred, used for drills and repeating vocabulary and grammar (Burston, 2014b).

Today, smartphones and tablets are considered essential devices in the language classroom (Zhang & Zou, 2022). They can improve language learning (Wong & Looi, 2010) by increasing the time learners spend on it outside of class (Burston, 2015) and supporting communication among them (Zhang & Zou, 2022). Learners can use them to access materials, create and share digital content, and hold virtual discussions with their classmates (Morgana, 2019). For example, they can communicate with teachers using specific writing apps, collaboratively read the same e-books, write a manuscript synchronously using an e-book creator, or publish and share a book online using Twitter or Instagram. Smartphones and tablets also allow learners to access learning activities as needed, make video recordings, take pictures, and connect with classmates in other locations (Almaiah & Mulhem, 2019). Microlearning (i.e. learning delivered in bite-sized chunks) can also be delivered through mobile devices.

2.3   Theories

Theories help us understand how learning happens and inform practice. Many theories and methods applied in the literature on CALL and MALL were developed in the late 19th and early twentieth centuries. Scholars who research the use of technology in language learning often apply theories from applied linguistics but also embrace psychology, learning theories, and instructional design (e.g. Hubbard, 2009). CALL and MALL have occasionally been criticized for lack of theoretical rigour (Li, 2018), as not all research studies addressing them are grounded in theory (Hubbard, 2009).

However, researchers may not mention minor theoretical contributions; however, this does not imply that theory is irrelevant to their research.

2.4   Sociocultural Theory of Learning

Activity theory and Vygotsky's (1978) sociocultural theory of learning have informed MALL research on collaboration and experiential and social learning (Burnside & Muilenburg, 2012; Neumann & Neumann, 2014). Perhaps the key concept adopted from Vygotsky is that social interaction is essential in learning and development. Vygotsky argued that learning occurs in a "zone of proximal development" (ZPD). In MALL, this refers to the interactions between the learner, teacher, and mobile devices. In other words, mobile devices play a crucial role in meaning-making (Viberg & Grönlund, 2012). For example, it is possible to augment social interaction using interactive virtual environments, such as Second Life (Wang et al., 2013).

Another key concept in Vygotsky's (1978) sociocultural theory is personalization. This refers to learner choice, autonomy, and agency. Learners enjoy a higher degree of agency when they use mobile devices. In addition, teachers can design different activities to meet learners' individual needs, preferences, and learning methods (Viberg & Grönlund, 2012). Activities and tools can also be adjusted to different confidence levels (e.g. beginner, intermediate) and scaffolding (a feature of the ZPD) can help ESL/EFL learners develop (Lantolf, 2000, 2006). By designing differentiated activities that can be delivered via mobile devices, teachers can foster ESL/EFL learners' proficiency (Li, 2017).

2.5   Noticing Hypothesis

Mobile devices allow teachers to assign activities that support the noticing hypothesis, which posits that learners need ample opportunities to notice new linguistic features in the target language as this increases awareness, comprehension, and acquisition (Schmidt, 2010). For example, learners can identify new vocabulary words and write them down (Kukulska-Hulme & Bull, 2009). Later, they can use this vocabulary to support their studies by completing learning activities and practising output. Teacher-designed activities based on the noticing hypothesis can help learners store information in their long-term memory and increase their awareness; these processes support the later processing of language (Schmidt, 1995).

Mobile microlearning can integrate the noticing process in English language acquisition. For example, noticing a new language element and noting it is an example of bite-sized learning. Then, the learner can use their mobile device to access follow-up checklists or infographics with additional support to fill any gaps and support the retention of new knowledge (Craik & Lockhart, 1972). This enables language learners to produce meaningful and comprehensive output (Swain, 2006).

2.6 Self-regulated Learning

Self-regulated learning (SRL) refers to learners' ability to manage and monitor their thoughts and behaviours during the learning process (Pintrich, 2004). It is associated with success in various contexts (Muller & Seufert, 2018). Learners who can plan, manage, and control their learning processes learn faster and outperform others (Kizilcec et al., 2017). In microlearning, which requires learners to complete bite-sized learning activities, learners must be able to self-regulate so they can move naturally from one activity to another and improve their performance.

Another important aspect of SRL is perceived learning (PL), which comprises three main dimensions: cognitive, emotional, and social. The cognitive aspect refers to the acquisition of new knowledge through the learning process ('I know'). The emotional aspect relates to the subjective feelings involved in the learning process (e.g. difficulty, enjoyment) and includes the attitudes that students develop while learning the course content. Finally, the social aspect of PL refers to enjoying one's interactions with one's peers or teachers during the learning process (Blau et al., 2017). It is important to consider SRL and PL when designing and optimizing microlearning activities for ESL/EFL learners.

2.7 Reflection Questions

1. What roles do you think technology and microlearning will play in the future of language learning?
2. How has the introduction of mobile devices impacted language learning?
3. What are some potential drawbacks or limitations of mobile microlearning?
4. How can personalization and collaboration be integrated into MALL activities?
5. How can the noticing hypothesis be applied to microlearning activities for language acquisition?

2.8 Conclusion

The use of technology in language education has evolved over the years, from the use of mainframe computers for repetitive drills to the integration of multimedia and the internet to facilitate acquisition. The emergence of mobile devices has given rise to MALL, which allows learners to acquire language anytime and anywhere. Personalization, collaboration, and experiential and social forms of learning are some of the principles that inform mobile microlearning.

References

Almaiah, M. A., & Al Mulhem, A. (2019). Analysis of the essential factors affecting of intention to use of mobile learning applications: A comparison between universities adopters and non-adopters. *Education and Information Technologies, 24*(2), 1433–1468. https://doi.org/10.1007/s10639-018-9840-1

Blau, I., Weiser, O., & Eshet-Alkalai, Y. (2017). How do medium naturalness and personality traits shape academic achievement and perceived learning? An experimental study of face-to-face and synchronous e-learning. *Research in Learning Technology, 25*. Retrieved from https://eric.ed.gov/?id=EJ1163190

Burnside, R., & Muilenburg, L. (2012). Using the iPad to support early struggling readers. *In EdMedia+ innovate learning* (pp. 2374–2375). Association for the Advancement of Computing in Education (AACE).

Burston, J. (2014a). MALL: The pedagogical challenges. *Computer Assisted Language Learning, 27*(4), 344–357. https://doi.org/10.1080/09588221.2014.914539

Burston, J. (2014b). The reality of MALL project implementations: Still on the fringes. *CALICO Journal, 31*(1), 43–65. https://doi.org/10.11139/cj.31.1.103-125

Burston, J. (2015). Twenty years of MALL project implementation: A meta-analysis of learning outcomes. *ReCALL, 27*(1), 4–20. https://doi.org/10.1017/S0958344014000159

Chapelle, C. (2001). *Computer applications in second language acquisition: Foundations for teaching, testing, and research.* Cambridge University Press.

Chun, D. (2016). The role of technology in SLA research. *Language Learning & Technology, 20*(2), 98–115. Retrieved from http://llt.msu.edu/issues/june2016/chun.pdf

Chun, D. (2019). Current and future directions in TELL. *Educational Technology & Society, 22*(2), 14–25. Retrieved from https://drive.google.com/file/d/1N1wWPNx8g0CAHki8s01iGNsgGqZttRyg/view

Craik, F. I. M., & Lockhart, R. S. (1972). Levels of processing: A framework for memory research 1. *Journal of Verbal Learning and Verbal Behavior, 11*(6), 671–684. https://doi.org/10.1016/S0022-5371(72)80001-X

Hubbard, P. (2009). Developing CALL theory: A new frontier. In M. Thomas (Ed.), *New frontiers in CALL: Negotiating diversity* (pp. 1–6). JALT CALL SIG.

Kizilcec, R. F., Perez-Sanagustin, M., & Maldonado, J. J. (2017). Self-regulated learning strategies predict learner behavior and goal attainment in Massive Open Online Courses. *Computers & Education, 14*, 18–33. https://doi.org/10.1016/j.compedu.2016.10.001

Kohnke, L. (2020). Exploring learner perception, experience and motivation of using a mobile app in L2 vocabulary acquisition. *International Journal of Computer-Assisted Language Learning and Teaching, 10*(1), 15–26. https://doi.org/10.4018/IJCALLT.2020010102

Kohnke, L. (2021). GoSoapBox—Encourage participation and interaction in the language classroom. *RELC Journal, 52*(3), 648–650. https://doi.org/10.1177/0033688219872570

Kohnke, L., & Moorhouse, B. L. (2021). Using Kahoot! To gamify learning in the language classroom. *RELC Journal (OnlineFirst).* https://doi.org/10.1177/00336882211040270

Kukulska-Hulme, A., & Bull, S. (2009). Theory-based support for mobile language learning: Noticing and recording. *International Journal of Interactive Mobile Technologies (iJIM), 3*(2), 12–18. https://doi.org/10.3991/ijim.v3i2.7

Kukulska-Hulme, A., & Shield, L. (2008). An overview of mobile assisted language learning: From content delivery to supported collaboration and interaction. *ReCALL, 20*(3), 271–289. https://doi.org/10.1017/S0958344008000335

Lantolf, J. P. (2000). Second language learning as a mediated process. *Language Teaching, 33*(2), 79–96. https://doi.org/10.1017/S0261444800015329

Lantolf, J. P. (2006). Sociocultural theory and L2: State of the art. *Studies in Second Language Acquisition, 28*(1), 67–109. https://doi.org/10.1017/S0272263106060037

Levy, M. (2000). *CALL context and conceptualization.* Oxford University Press.

Li, J. (2018). Digital affordances on WeChat: Learning Chinese as a second language. *Computer Assisted Language Learning, 31*(1–2), 27–52. https://doi.org/10.1080/09588221.2017.1376687

Li, L. (2017). *New technologies and language learning.* Routledge.

Liu, P. L., & Chen, C. J. (2015). Learning English through actions: A study of mobile assisted language learning. *Interactive Learning Environments, 23*(2), 158–171. https://doi.org/10.1080/10494820.2014.959976

Moorhouse, B. L., & Kohnke, L. (2020). Using Mentimeter to elicit student responses in the EAP/ESP classroom. *RELC Journal, 51*(1), 198–204. https://doi.org/10.1177/0033688219890350

Morgana, V. (2019). A review of MALL: From categories to implementation. The case of Apple's iPad. *The EuroCALL Review, 27*(2), 1–12.

Morgana, V., & Kukulska-Hulme, A. (2021). *Mobile-assisted language learning across educational contexts.* Routledge.

Müller, N. M., & Seufert, T. (2018). Effects of self-regulation prompts in hypermedia learning on learning performance and self-efficacy. *Learning and Instruction, 58*, 1–11. https://doi.org/10.1016/j.learninstruc.2018.04.011

Neumann, M. M., & Neumann, D. L. (2014). Touch screen tablets and emergent literacy. *Early Childhood Education Journal, 42*(4), 231–239. https://doi.org/10.1007/s10643-013-0608-3

Pintrich, P. R. (2004). A conceptual framework for assessing motivation and self-regulated learning in college students. *Educational Psychology Review, 16*, 385–407. https://doi.org/10.1007/s10648-004-0006-x

Schmidt, R. (1995). Consciousness and foreign language learning: A tutorial on the role of attention and awareness in learning. In R. Schmidt (Ed.), *Attention and awareness in foreign language learning* (pp. 1–63). University of Hawaii, Second Language Teaching & Curriculum Center.

Schmidt, R. (2010). Attention, awareness, and individual differences in language learning. In W. M. Chan, S. Chi, K. N. Cin, J. Istanto, M. Nagami, J. W. Sew, T. Suthiwan, & I. Walker (Eds.), *Proceedings of CLaSIC 2010,* Singapore, December 2–4 (pp. 721–737). National University of Singapore, Centre for Language Studies.

Swain, M. (2006). Languaging, agency and collaboration in advanced second language proficiency. In H. Byrnes (Ed.), *Advanced language learning: The contribution of Halliday and Vygotsky* (pp. 95–108). Continuum.

Viberg, O., & Grönlund, Å. (2012). Mobile assisted language learning: A literature review. In *Proceedings of the 11th International Conference on Mobile and Contextual Learning,* Helsinki (pp. 1–8).

Vygotsky, L. S. (1978). Mind in society. In *The development of higher psychological processes.* Harvard University Press.

Wang, A., Deutschmann, M., & Steinvall, A. (2013). Towards a model for mapping participation: Exploring factors affecting participation in a telecollaborative learning scenario in Second Life. *The JALT CALL Journal, 9*(1), 3–22.

Warschauer, M. (2004). Technological change and the future of CALL. In S. Fotos & C. Brown (Eds.), *New perspectives on CALL for second and foreign language classrooms* (pp. 15–25). Lawrence Erlbaum Associates.

Wong, L. H., & Looi, C. K. (2010). Vocabulary learning by mobile-assisted authentic content creation and social meaning-making: Two case studies. *Journal of Computer Assisted Learning, 26*(5), 421–433. https://doi.org/10.1111/j.1365-2729.2010.00357.x

Zhang, R., & Zou, D. (2022). Types, purposes, and effectiveness of state-of-the-art technologies for second and foreign language learning. *Computer Assisted Language Learning, 35*(4), 696–742. https://doi.org/10.1080/09588221.2020.1744666

Chapter 3
Practical Strategies to Optimize Mobile Microlearning

Abstract This chapter introduces four key strategies to optimize microlearning using mobile devices, relating to learner needs, medium, interactivity, and simplicity. It also introduces possible tools and applications one can use and the principles of designing microlearning lessons.

Keywords Microlearning · Practical strategies · Learner needs · Medium · Simplicity · Tools and applications

3.1 Practical Strategies

The aim of microlearning is to develop simple and well-structured content using high-impact, media-rich content, allowing learners to understand the content efficiently and effectively (Zhang & Ren, 2011). When mobile devices are incorporated, microlearning lessons can be made available anytime and anywhere (Sun et al., 2015), so that learners can review previous content or acquire new information without experiencing information overload. To ensure that this content is easy to absorb, microlearning lessons must be designed meaningfully and effectively.

The following elements are essential: the incorporation of videos, animations and other visual components; minimal text; responsive page designs; and consistent and recurrent elements. It is key to keep all aspects easy to navigate and digest by including only what is necessary for the task. By remembering that less is more, we can facilitate the effective transmission and retention of information.

Microlearning requires high-quality content to be as effective as traditional pedagogical approaches. We should strive to make the content visual, interactive, and straightforward. In addition, the learning objectives should be focused and specific (Bratt, 2020) because the goal is to achieve short and effective bursts of learning. For example, a textbook can be divided into small, manageable chunks—learning events—that can be delivered via mobile devices. For example, a lesson could begin with a 2-min animated video that provides an overview of the topic, followed by a 4-min flashcard activity in which learners drill new vocabulary words and then read a paragraph in an e-book. Finally, learners could access an infographic to help them remember the main points of the story, vocabulary, and other relevant information (Kohnke & Jarvis, 2023). When segmenting content for mobile microlearning, it is crucial to ensure that each activity has a single, manageable learning goal. We should consider these questions:

- What is the learning aim?
- How will microlearning help learners achieve this aim?
- What forms of multimodality should be employed?

Answering these questions will help teachers determine how to structure mobile learning content. In addition, to create effective microlearning lessons, it is important to consider learners' needs, the medium, interactivity and simplicity.

3.2   Learner Needs

Microlearning is about meeting the needs of today's learners and delivering personalized, flexible learning in bite-sized chunks (Kohnke & Foung, in-press). Therefore, when considering how to create microlearning activities, it is first necessary to think about learners' needs and how they can be met through mobile activities. We should also focus on optimizing the use of learners' time. The specific approach to adopt will depend on the following factors:

- What do learners need to know?
- What resources will they find useful?
- How will it affect their learning?

After answering these questions, the next step is to decide on the objective. Is the purpose of the activity to prepare learners for the next class or to reinforce the content of previous class discussions? Or do you want to create a standalone activity? When designing an activity, we must carefully consider learners' needs and how they will apply their learning to increase the likelihood that they achieve the learning outcomes. Finally, teachers need to consider how the microlearning activities will affect their capacity as facilitators of knowledge. Will the activity enrich learning and supplement existing materials—or will it waste time and/or impede existing pedagogical practice?

3.3   Medium

Many forms of media can be used in microlearning activities. Video is often the preferred medium as it can be used to combine text, audio, and graphics to increase explanatory power. However, many other options are available, such as social media, infographics, podcasts, augmented reality, virtual reality, and PDFs, and each of these appeals to a different type of learner. It is important to keep the design of the activities simple and ensure that the technology does not overpower the content or distract learners. When considering which medium is most suitable for delivering the content, it is essential to ask:

- What medium or format is most relevant and specific to the topic?
- What should learners do before, during, and after the event?

We should avoid using too many different learning elements (e.g. audio, animations, quizzes, slideshows, PDFs, and links) within a single activity. One benefit of microlearning is that it prevents cognitive overload; learners do not get confused if a lesson is short and focused. Finally, each activity must come with instructions that explain the concept, summarize the key points, and provide resources with further information.

3.4 Interactivity

Interactivity and engagement are vital to ensure that learners participate actively in microlearning. As the activities are short, learners must be focused, interested, and motivated to complete them. One effective strategy to achieve this is to embed various features in the chosen medium to appeal to different learning styles and preferences, especially those that reduce levels of passivity and increase output. For example, activities could incorporate:

- Single or multiple-choice questions
- Branching for learning decisions
- Dropdown lists
- 'Fill in the blank' exercises
- 'Click and reveal' exercises.

To ensure that activities are simple, short, and effective, we should always focus on the learning objectives and consider how each feature will help learners achieve the desired outcome. One effective strategy is to include digital flashcards at the end of an activity so learners can review the main points. Adding an interactive self-assessment checklist for learners can help the teacher determine whether they have grasped the content. Alternatively, learners could be asked to write a short reflection and post it on social media or the class blog to demonstrate their learning (Kohnke, 2019).

3.5 Simplicity

Microlearning should be clear, targeted, and focused; simplicity is key. Therefore, concepts should be presented one step at a time (Lindner, 2007), be easy to digest, deliver immediate learning/results, and hold learners' attention. To achieve simplicity, consider the intended audience and the best way to present the information without dumbing it down.

Significantly, simplicity does not mean that microlearning does not require learners to master complex knowledge or skills. Instead, the fundamental premise is that each *activity* remains simple, although the *content* evolves from simple to complex. Each activity should have a single purpose and learning objective that contribute to the larger aim of the course. Therefore, when it is necessary to teach more complex concepts, we should do so by developing a series of simple activities (e.g. video/animation tutorials, self-checklists, quizzes).

These four considerations should always be kept in mind when designing and optimizing practical microlearning activities for mobile devices. Microlearning is not about 'dumbing down' teaching and learning materials. Instead, it is about motivating learners and ensuring that they actively engage in meaningful learning while using mobile devices (Hwang & Chen, 2017). These practical strategies are particularly well-suited to the learning capabilities and skills of the current generation of learners (Aitchanov et al., 2018; Dai et al., 2018) and can enhance learning among EFL/ESL students (Kohnke & Foung, in-press). Of course, microlearning is not a one-size-fits-all strategy, so these approaches should be considered carefully and implemented when they are appropriate based on the teacher's judgment.

3.6 Tools and Applications

Mobile learning and multisensory applications provide flexible and timely opportunities to learn. They use audio, text, and visual elements to explain, complement, and clarify learning content. For teachers, it is often challenging to decide which applications to use. A good point of reference is to consider the following questions:

- How do I find high-quality applications?
- Which applications are good aids for learning about this subject?
- Which learning applications do learners already use and like?

Selecting the most suitable app for delivering microlearning activities is paramount for making the tasks useful and engaging while deepening the learning process. Applications should be easy to access, set up, and use; they should also motivate learners to complete the activities (Nikou & Economides, 2018a, 2018b). Teachers should aim to use applications that allow them to create or modify activities (e.g. checklists, word clouds). Because these tasks are more personalized, learners may find them more engaging and thus are more likely to complete them.

3.7   Design Principles

The crucial principle to remember when designing microlearning activities is that each lesson should centre on a single learning objective or topic. The activity should be driven by learner engagement (clicking and progressing through the learning materials) rather than the creation of artefacts or products (Cerratto-Pragman & Jahnke, 2019). The following structure is suggested:

1. Introduction that showcases the relevance of the topic
2. Interactive content
3. Short exercises
4. Instant feedback.

See sample activity 1 for an example of a mobile microlearning activity that follows this structure.

3.8   Sample Activity

Topic: Effective email communication.
Objective: To identify the key elements of an effective email.

Introduction: An animated video provides a brief overview of effective email communication.

Interactive content: An infographic highlights the subject line, tone, grammar, punctuation, and formatting.

Short exercise: A fill-in-the-blank exercise allows learners to apply the concepts of effective email communication.

Instant feedback: The fill-in-the-blank exercise includes automatic feedback, explaining why certain answers are correct or incorrect.

This activity focuses on a single learning objective, identifying the key elements of effective email communication. It is structured to be very brief and engaging, with interactive elements that reinforce learning and engage learners to apply their new knowledge.

According to Jonassen (1996), learning design should prioritize learning *from* technologies (e.g. 'listen and watch' instructional materials) rather than *with* them (e.g. create projects to demonstrate learning). To achieve this, the content should be concise and easy to absorb, and the correct answers should be readily available. However, teachers should also consider the possible costs for learners, as some may not own mobile devices or have unlimited access to high-speed internet. It is also essential to keep in mind that mobile devices have limited screen space and ensure that the flow of information is simple, practical, and tailored to learners' needs. The following four chapters describe tools, applications, and software that are user-friendly and require little technical knowledge, as well as activities that can enhance ESL/EFL learning.

3.9 Conclusion

Teachers must be equipped with the right technical and content knowledge to design microlearning activities that support the learning of ESL/EFL students. This chapter has presented four key considerations for optimizing mobile microlearning and a four-stage structure for microlearning activities. By engaging in short bursts of learning, each with a single purpose, learners can master complex knowledge and skills.

References

Aitchanov, B., Zhaparov, M., & Ibragimov, M. (2018). The research and development of the information system on mobile devices for micro-learning in educational institutes. In *14th International Conference on Electronics Computer and Computation (ICECCO)* (pp. 1–4). IEEE.

Bratt, S. (2020). *Essential strategies for developing mobile-based micro-learning.* Edmedia + Innovate Learning Proceeding. Association for the Advancement of Computing in Education (AACE).

Cerratto-Pragman, T., & Jahnke, I. (2019). *Emergent practices and material conditions in learning and teaching with technologies.* Springer.

Dai, H., Tao, Y., & Shi, T. W. (2018). Research on mobile learning and micro course in the big data environment. In *Proceedings of the 2nd International Conference on e-Education, e-Business and e-Technology* (pp. 48–51). ACM.

Hwang, G.-J., & Chen, C.-H. (2017). Influences of an inquiry-based ubiquitous gaming design on students' learning achievements, motivation, behavioral patterns, and tendency towards critical thinking and problem solving. *British Journal of Educational Technology, 48,* 950–971. https://doi.org/10.1111/bjet.12464

Jonassen, D. H. (1996). *Computers in the classroom: Mindtools for critical thinking.* Prentice-Hall, Inc.

Kohnke, L. (2019). Use sticky-notes and make the content stick. *Teacher Trainer, 33*(1), 6–7.

Kohnke, L., & Foung, F. (in-press). Exploring microlearning for CALL teacher education and professional development: Voices from Hong Kong. In D. Tafazoli, & M. Picard (Eds.), *CALL teacher education and professional development: Voices from under-represented context* (pp. xx–xx). Springer.

Kohnke, L., & Jarvis, A. (2023). Developing infographics for English for academic purposes courses. *TESOL Journal, 14*(1), 1–5. https://doi.org/10.1002/tesj.675

Lindner, M. (2007). What is microlearning? (Introductory note). In *3rd International Microlearning 2007 Conference.* Innsbruck University Press.

Nikou, S., & Economides, A. (2018a). Mobile-based assessment: A literature review of publications in major referred journals from 2009 to 2018. *Computers & Education, 125,* 101–119. https://doi.org/10.1016/j.compedu.2018.06.006

Nikou, S., & Economides, A. (2018b). Mobile-based micro-learning and assessment: Impact on learning performance and motivation of high school students. *Journal of Computer Assisted Learning, 34*(3), 269–278. https://doi.org/10.1111/jcal.12240

Sun, G., Cui, T., Yong, J, Shen, J., & Chen, S. (2015). Drawing micro learning into MOOC: Using fragmented pieces of time to enable eBective entire course learning experiences. In *International Conference on Computer Supported Cooperative Work in Design* (pp. 308–313). IEEE CPS.

Zhang, X., & Ren, L. (2011). Design for application of micro learning to informal training in enterprise. In *2nd International Conference on Artificial Intelligence, Management Science and Electronic Commerce* (pp. 2024–2027). https://doi.org/10.1109/AIMSEC.2011.6011235

Chapter 4
Mobile Microlearning: Enhancing Listening, Speaking, Writing, and Reading Skills

Abstract This chapter demonstrates how microlearning lessons can improve the four primary language skills—listening, speaking, writing, and reading—and provides examples of each.

Keywords Microlearning · Listening · Speaking · Writing · Reading · Collaborative learning

4.1 Listening

Effective listening skills are crucial for ESL/EFL learners. Listening provides learners with comprehensive input, which is essential for language acquisition (Krashen, 1982). Learners acquire language when they can grasp the meaning of what they hear, even if they do not understand every word. Listening exposes learners to new vocabulary and grammatical structures, which helps them to internalize these features and use them more effectively in their speech and writing (Nation, 2001).

Listening activities also expose learners to authentic language, which allows them to develop their understanding and fluency over time. When listening to native and near-native speakers, learners encounter authentic speech patterns, which helps them to notice differences between their speech and those of the other speakers. This allows them to adjust and improve their pronunciation (Celce-Murcia et al., 2010). In the process, learners develop a more natural-sounding accent and learn to pronounce words and phrases correctly.

Moreover, learners first recognize and identify sounds, words, and phrases through listening (Brown, 2017). Developing listening comprehension is essential for learners who must understand spoken English to engage in social, academic, and professional communication (Goh & Vandergrift, 2022). Listening also facilitates the development of critical thinking skills in learners (Bond, 2012). They learn to identify primary concepts, draw inferences, and formulate conclusions from what they hear (Jarvis et al., 2020).

Microlearning on mobile devices allows learners to improve their listening skills in different contexts. For example, they can listen to short podcasts or audio clips covering many topics, narrated by speakers with various accents. This material may include debates, interviews, and short stories. Teachers can construct playlists or propose certain episodes for learners to access whenever they are available, including while commuting. Teachers can use the following classroom learning activities as written or modify them to suit their needs.

4.1.1   Listening Activity 1

Title: Listening Ladder: Recognizing Sounds, Words, and Phrases
Objective: To improve learners' listening skills by helping them recognize and identify sounds, words, and phrases
Level: Elementary
Duration: 6 min
Materials Needed: A set of prerecorded audio clips featuring different sounds, words, and phrases (e.g. environmental sounds, everyday vocabulary, simple sentences)

Preparation: Prepare a set of prerecorded audio clips. To make this a mobile microlearning activity, create a digital list using an application (Padlet, Lino), website, or audio player that learners can access on their mobile devices. Examples include environmental sounds (e.g. doorbell, dog barking), everyday vocabulary (e.g. "an apple", "book"), or simple sentences (e.g. "I have a dog", "What day is it?").

Learner Practice:

1. *Individual Practice (2 min)*: Share the audio clips with the learners. Ask them to listen to the clips individually using their mobile devices, focusing on recognizing the sounds, words, and phrases they hear.
2. *Pair Discussion (2 min)*: After learners have listened to the audio clips, ask them to pair up with a partner. (If the activity is conducted remotely, use a mobile application or platform supporting breakout rooms or private messaging.) The pairs discuss the audio clips they hear, comparing their answers and collaborating to identify any sounds, words, or phrases they missed.

3. *Check Answers/Feedback (2 min)*: Review the audio clips and confirm the correct answers as a large group. Ask learners to reflect on their performance.

Follow-up: With their partners, students could reflect on any challenges they faced while identifying the sounds, words, and phrases, and share strategies for improvement.

4.1.2 Listening Activity 2

Title: Academic Audio Snapshots: Listening Comprehension for Intermediate Learners
Objective: To improve learners' listening comprehension by helping them understand spoken academic English through short audio excerpts
Level: Intermediate
Duration: 4 min
Materials Needed: A set of prerecorded audio excerpts from academic lectures or presentations (approximately 30 s each)

Preparation: Prepare a set of prerecorded audio excerpts from academic lectures or presentations appropriate for intermediate learners. To make this a mobile microlearning activity, create a digital list using an application (Padlet, Lino), website, or audio player that learners can access on their mobile devices. Ensure that audio excerpts are clear and high-quality.

Learner Practice:

1. *Individual Practice (1 min)*: Share the audio excerpts with the learners. Ask them to listen to the excerpts individually using their mobile devices, focusing on understanding the main ideas and supporting details. Learners

should try to comprehend as much information as possible within the allocated time.

2. *Pair Discussion (1 min)*: After learners have listened to the audio excerpts, ask them to pair up with a partner. (If the activity is conducted remotely, use a mobile application or platform supporting breakout rooms or private messaging.) In pairs, learners discuss the content of the audio excerpts, comparing their understanding and collaborating to fill in any gaps in comprehension.

3. *Check Answers/Feedback (2 min)*: As a large group, ask the learners to reflect on their performance, review the audio excerpts, and confirm the main ideas and supporting details.

Follow-up: Ask learners to reflect on any challenges they faced while comprehending spoken academic English and share strategies for improvement.

4.1.3 Listening Activity 3

Title: Listening Detectives: Developing Critical Thinking Skills
Objective: To improve learners' listening skills and critical thinking ability by identifying key information and making inferences
Level: Beginner
Duration: 5 min
Materials Needed: A prerecorded audio story or dialogue appropriate for beginner learners, featuring clear language and a simple narrative

Preparation: Prepare a prerecorded audio story or dialogue with clear language, a simple narrative, and different characters or speakers.

Learner Practice:

1. *Individual Listening (1 min)*: Share the audio story or dialogue with learners. Ask them to listen individually using their mobile devices and focus on understanding the main ideas and identifying key information.
2. *Pair Discussion (2 min)*: After learners have listened to the audio, ask them to pair up with a partner. (If the activity is conducted remotely, use a mobile application or platform supporting breakout rooms or private messaging). In pairs, learners discuss the content of the audio, focusing on the following critical thinking tasks:

   - identifying the main ideas and key information
   - making inferences about the characters, setting, or events in the story or dialogue
   - predicting what might happen in the story or dialogue

3. *Check Answer/Feedback (2 min)*: Review the audio story or dialogue as a group and share answers.

Follow-up: Ask learners to reflect on their critical thinking abilities and challenges while listening and making inferences.

These listening activities encourage learners to practice listening skills by identifying and recognizing sounds, words, and phrases. The learners participate in individual, pair, and group discussions to improve their listening skills, gain confidence, and learn to think critically about the information they hear.

4.2 Speaking

Speaking is vital for ESL/EFL learners to acquire the language since it enables them to produce language. Swain's (1995) output hypothesis proposes that producing linguistic output enables learners to identify knowledge gaps, experiment with new forms, and formulate hypotheses about the language, all of which encourage development. In addition, speaking practice helps learners to improve their pronunciation, intonation, and fluency. Regular speaking opportunities also allow learners to refine their pronunciation and rhythm, leading to more natural-sounding speech (Derwing & Munro, 2005). By engaging in authentic speaking activities, learners practise using English in various contexts and for different purposes (Canale & Swain, 1980), which enables them to interact with others in the real world. Conversational interactions also allow learners to negotiate meaning, receive feedback, and modify their output (Long, 1996).

In addition, speaking practice increases confidence. When language learners engage in conversation regularly, they feel more at ease expressing their ideas, thoughts, and opinions in the target language. This enhanced confidence can result in more effective communication and enhanced linguistic abilities (MacIntyre & Gardner, 1991). In addition, learners receive immediate feedback from their teachers and peers, which helps them to identify and remedy errors (Lyster & Ranta, 1997). Lastly, improving their speaking abilities allows learners to participate in social activities and build friendships and professional relationships, which foster a sense of belonging and well-being (Dörnyei & Murphy, 2003).

To summarize, learners can gain confidence, receive vital feedback, and enjoy the benefits of social contact through speaking practice. The following are three examples of activities that build speaking skills and enhance communication abilities.

4.2.1 *Speaking Activity 1*

Title: Describe and Guess: Everyday Objects
Objective: To improve learners' speaking skills by encouraging them to describe objects in a fun and engaging way
Level: Any
Duration: 5 min
Materials Needed: A list of everyday objects (e.g. pen, chair, refrigerator, bicycle)

Preparation: Before starting the activity, prepare a list of 10–12 everyday objects that learners likely know. To make this a mobile microlearning activity, create a digital list using an application (Padlet, Lino), website, or document (Google Docs) that learners can access using their mobile devices.

Learner Practice:

1. *Pair Up (1 min)*: Ask learners to pair up with a partner. If the activity is conducted remotely, use a mobile application or platform supporting breakout rooms or private messaging.

2. *Describe and Guess (2 min)*: In pairs, learners take turns describing an object from the list without saying the word. They should use clear, detailed descriptions to help their partner guess the object based on the description. Once the object is guessed correctly or after 30 s (whichever comes first), learners switch roles. (Example description: "This object is found in a kitchen. It's usually white, and it keeps food cold. It is sometimes attached to a freezer." Answer: refrigerator).

3. *Pair Reflection (2 min)*: After completing the activity, ask learners to reflect on their performance. In pairs, they should discuss any challenges they faced while describing or guessing the objects and share strategies for improvement.

Alternative: To make the activity more difficult, ask the learners to describe objects without using certain words (e.g. describe "bicycle" without using "wheel" or "ride").

4.2.2 Speaking Activity 2

Title: Phonetic Fun: Practising Pronunciation, Intonation, and Fluency
Objective: To improve learners' speaking skills, focusing on pronunciation, intonation, and fluency in a structured and engaging manner
Level: Any
Duration: 6 min
Materials Needed: A list of target words or phrases that focus on specific challenges related to pronunciation or intonation (e.g. minimal pairs, homophones, idiomatic expressions)

Preparation: Prepare a list of target words or phrases that offer specific pronunciation or intonation challenges. For a mobile microlearning activity, create a digital list using an application (Padlet, Lino), website, or document (Google Docs) that learners can access using their mobile devices. Examples of target words or phrases include minimal pairs (e.g. "ship" vs "sheep"), homophones (e.g. "there" vs "their" vs "they're"), or idiomatic expressions (e.g. "break a leg" or "piece of cake").

Learner Practice:

1. *Group Formation (1 min)*: Divide learners into groups of 3–4. If the activity is conducted remotely, use a mobile application or platform supporting breakout rooms or group messaging.
2. *Modelling (1 min)*: Share the list of target words or phrases with the learners. Model the correct pronunciation and intonation of each word or phrase, and ask learners to listen carefully and repeat after you.
3. *Pronunciation Relay (3 min)*: In their groups, learners take turns saying the target word or phrases. The first learner says a word or phrase from the list, focusing on accurate pronunciation and intonation. The next learner repeats it, trying to mimic the first learner's pronunciation and intonation as closely as possible. This process continues until all learners in the group have repeated the word or phrase. Then, the group moves on to the next item on the list.
4. *Group Reflection (1 min)*: After completing the activity, ask learners to reflect on their performance.

Follow-up: In their groups, learners could discuss pronunciation, intonation, or fluency problems and share ways to fix them. At this point, the teacher can also give feedback.

4.2.3 Speaking Activity 3

Title: Context Carousel: Practising English for Different Purposes
Objective: To improve learners' speaking skills by asking them to use English in various contexts and adapt their language for different purposes and audiences
Level: Any
Duration: 6 min

Materials Needed: A list of contextual prompts designed to elicit conversations about the different situations, purposes, or audiences (e.g. giving directions to a tourist, ordering food at a restaurant, asking for help in a store, introducing oneself to a professional contact)

Preparation: Prepare a list of contextual prompts representing different situations, purposes, or audiences. For a mobile microlearning activity, create a digital list using an application (Padlet, Lino), website, or document (Google Docs) that learners can access using their mobile devices.

Learner Practice:

1. *Pair Up (1 min)*: Ask learners to pair up with a partner. If the activity is conducted remotely, use a mobile application or platform that supports breakout rooms or private messaging.
2. *Context Carousel (3 min)*: Give the learners the list of prompts. Learners take turns choosing a prompt and acting out a short role-play (approximately 30 s). They should pay attention to using the right words, tone, and register for the situation. After each role-play, the learners switch roles and choose a new question. (Example prompt: "You are a tourist asking a local for directions to a nearby landmark.")
3. *Pair Reflection (2 min)*: After completing the activity, ask learners to reflect on their performance.

Follow-up: In pairs, students talk about pronunciation, intonation, or fluency problems they had and share ways to fix them. At this point, the teacher also gives feedback.

These three activities encourage learners to practise adapting their language to different situations and audiences and give them valuable experience in using English effectively and appropriately. Their pronunciation, intonation, and fluency will improve, and they will become more aware of key aspects of spoken English.

4.3 Writing

Writing is another essential skill for ESL/EFL learners because they can produce more controlled and thoughtful language when writing than speaking. Writing encourages them to reflect on and revise their language use. They can evaluate their progress and develop metacognitive awareness (Hinkel, 2001). This allows them to better understand grammatical structures, vocabulary, and conventions (Hyland, 2003). Writing also allows learners to practise organizing their thoughts and expressing themselves coherently. This skill is required for completing assignments; writing research papers, emails, and reports; and creating clear, well-structured texts that communicate their intended messages to the reader (Grabe & Kaplan, 2014). By practising different genres, learners become more familiar with genre conventions and structures, allowing them to produce more authentic and effective texts (Paltridge, 2004). Learners can also receive feedback from their teachers and peers, which they can use to revise and improve their work. As a result, their language use becomes more accurate and effective (Hyland & Hyland, 2006).

Writing practice promotes self-evaluation and metacognitive awareness, making learners better writers. The following three activities demonstrate how this can be accomplished through microlearning.

4.3.1 Writing Activity 1

Title: Grammar Gurus: Practising Language Conventions
Objective: To improve learners' writing skills by having them practise conventions (e.g. capitalization, punctuation, basic grammar rules)
Level: Elementary
Duration: 6 min
Materials Needed: A simple writing prompt (e.g. favourite season), a mobile application or platform that supports collaborative writing (e.g. Google Docs, Padlet, or a chat platform)

Preparation: Choose a simple writing prompt that encourages learners to write a short paragraph or a few sentences. For a mobile microlearning activity, use a mobile application or platform that supports collaborative writing, such as Google Docs, Padlet, or a chat platform.

Learner Practice:

1. *Individual Writing (2 min)*: Share the writing prompt. Ask learners to write a short paragraph or a few sentences responding to the prompt using their mobile devices, focusing on correct capitalization, punctuation, and grammar.
2. *Peer Review (2 min)*: Learners exchange their work with a partner. If the activity is being conducted remotely, use a mobile application or platform that supports sharing and commenting on documents. Learners review each other's work in pairs, identifying errors in language conventions and suggesting corrections.
3. *Check Answers/Feedback (2 min)*: Review the writing and provide feedback.

Follow-up: Ask learners to reflect on the language conventions they practised and any challenges they encountered during the activity.

4.3.2 Writing Activity 2

Title: Practising Academic Sentence Structure
Objective: To improve learners' writing skills by having them practise academic sentence structure
Level: Intermediate
Duration: 5 min
Materials Needed: A list of 2–4 academic sentence starters,

Preparation: Create a list of 2–4 academic sentence starters that encourage learners to write compound or complex sentences. These sentences should include a mix of conjunctions and transitions suitable for intermediate learners. To make this a mobile microlearning activity, use a mobile application or platform that supports collaborative writing, such as Google Docs, Padlet, or a chat platform.

Learner Practice:

1. *Individual Writing (2 min)*: Share the list. Ask learners to use their mobile devices to choose one sentence starter and use it to create a complex or compound sentence that follows the conventions of academic sentence structure.
2. *Pair Discussion (2 min)*: Ask the learners to find a partner. Ask learners to share their sentences and discuss the academic sentence structures they used.
3. *Check Answer/Feedback (2 min)*: Review the sentences and provide feedback.

Follow-up: Ask learners to share their sentences with the class and reflect on their strategies to create academic sentences.

4.3.3 Writing Activity 3

Title: Writing Using Padlet
Objective: To improve learners' writing skills collaboratively
Level: Beginner, elementary, intermediate, advanced
Duration: 4 min
Materials Needed: Padlet, a simple story starter or prompt

Preparation:

1. Create a new Padlet board.
2. Select a simple story starter or prompt that encourages learners to write one sentence at a time to contribute to a collaborative story.
3. Add the story starter as the first story on the Padlet board.

Learner Practice:

1. *Individual Writing (2 min)*: Share the link to the Padlet boards. Ask learners to access the board using their mobile devices and write one sentence, either responding to the story starter or building on the previous sentence. They should add their sentence as a new post on the Padlet board.
2. *Group Check (2 min)*: Review the complete story together. Discuss the ideas and the flow of the story.

Follow-up: Ask learners to reflect on their experiences participating in the collaborative writing activity and any challenges they faced in contributing to the story.

These microlearning writing activities encourage learners of all levels to practise their writing skills in a supportive and engaging environment. Their understanding of academic conventions, sentence structure, and creative writing will improve.

4.4 Reading

Regular reading practice helps ESL/EFL learners develop reading fluency while exposing them to a wide range of vocabulary words, idiomatic expressions, and collocations (Taguchi et al., 2006). Learners who encounter new words in context can infer their meaning and gradually expand their lexicon (Nation, 2001). Contextual learning facilitates the internalization of grammar rules and language structures (Krashen, 1982). Reading also improves learners' comprehension and cognitive skills, including problem-solving, critical thinking, and information-processing skills (Grabe, 2009). Moreover, engaging with interesting texts can foster a sense of motivation and interest in learning English (Day & Bamford, 1998). Reading can also develop learners' listening and speaking skills indirectly. Applying the new vocabulary, expressions, and grammatical structures they encounter to listening and speaking activities results in more effective communication (Nuttall, 2005).

To summarize, learners can develop a solid foundation in the English language by engaging with authentic, diverse, and entertaining literature. The following activities will demonstrate how microlearning can be included in reading instruction.

4.4.1 Reading Activity 1

Title: Vocabulary Voyage: Encountering and Learning New Words in Context
Objective: To improve learners' reading skills and expand their vocabulary
Level: Beginner, elementary, intermediate, advanced
Duration: 6 min
Materials Needed: A short text or passage appropriate for the learners' level, featuring a mix of familiar and new vocabulary words

Preparation: To make this a mobile microlearning activity, create a digital list using an application (Padlet, Lino), website, or document (Google Docs) that learners can access using their mobile devices.

Learner Practice:

1. *Individual Reading (2 min)*: Share the text or passage with learners. Ask them to read the text individually using their mobile devices, focusing on understanding the main ideas and identifying new vocabulary words in context. Encourage learners to use context clues to guess the meaning of new words.
2. *Pair Discussion (2 min)*: After learners have read the text, ask them to pair up with a partner. Learners discuss the new vocabulary words they identified in pairs and share their guesses about the meaning based on the context. They should also discuss challenges they faced while reading and encountering new words. If the activity is conducted remotely, use a mobile application or platform supporting breakout rooms or private messaging.
3. *Check Answers/Feedback (2 min)*: Review the text or passage as a large group. Confirm the meaning of the new vocabulary words.

Follow-up: Ask learners to reflect on the strategies they used to figure out the meanings of the words in context.

4.4.2 Reading Activity 2

Title: Reading Riddles: Developing Problem-Solving Skills
Objective: To improve learners' reading skills and problem-solving abilities through decoding and solving riddles
Level: Beginner, elementary, intermediate, advanced
Duration: 6 min
Materials Needed: A set (3–4) of short riddles appropriate for the learners' level, featuring clear language and a mix of familiar vocabulary words

Preparation: Choose a set of short riddles (3–4) appropriate for learners' level, featuring clear language and a mix of familiar vocabulary words. For a mobile microlearning activity, you can create a digital list using a mobile application (Padlet, Lino), website, or document (Google Docs) that learners can access.

Learner Practice:

1. *Individual Reading (2 min)*: Share the riddles with the learners. Ask them to read the riddles individually using their mobile devices, focusing on understanding the language and identifying clues that could help them solve the riddles.
2. *Pair Discussion (2 min)*: Ask them to pair up with a partner. If the activity is conducted remotely, use a mobile application or platform supporting breakout rooms or private messaging. Learners discuss their ideas in pairs and work together to solve the riddles, using reading comprehension and problem-solving skills.
3. *Check Answer/Feedback (2 min)*: Review the riddles and confirm the correct answers.

Follow-up: Ask the learners to reflect on the problem-solving strategies they used in reading and decoding the riddles.

4.4.3   Reading Activity 3

Title: Info-Processor: Developing Information Processing Skills through Reading
Objective: To improve learners' reading skills and information-processing abilities
Level: Beginner, elementary, intermediate, advanced
Duration: 5 min
Materials Needed: A short informational text or passage appropriate to the learners' level, featuring a mix of familiar and new vocabulary words

Preparation: Choose a short informational text or passage appropriate for the learners' level, featuring a mix of familiar and new vocabulary words. For a mobile microlearning activity, create a digital list using an application (Padlet, Lino), website, or document (Google Docs) that learners can access using their mobile devices.

Learner Practice:

1. *Individual Reading (2 min)*: Share the informational text or passage. Ask learners to read the text individually using their mobile devices, focusing on the main ideas and structure and identifying information.
2. *Organizing Information (1 min)*: Ask learners to create a simple outline or list on their mobile devices to organize the key information in the text. They should use the text structure as a guide to help them organize the information effectively.
3. *Check Answers/Feedback (2 min)*: Review the text or passage and discuss the outlines or lists that the learners made.

Follow-up: Ask learners to reflect on their information-processing strategies while reading and creating outlines/lists.

Individual reading and pair and group discussions can improve learners' reading comprehension and vocabulary skills in an engaging, fun, supportive, and collaborative environment.

4.5 Collaborative Spaces

The activities presented in this chapter are conducive to collaborative learning, which offers a range of benefits to ESL/EFL students.

- Collaborative learning provides opportunities for learners to engage in social interaction. Through discussions and negations, they can practice their language skills and receive immediate feedback from their peers (Long, 1996).
- Collaborative learning makes learning more enjoyable and fosters a sense of community that can encourage learners to be more actively involved (Dörnyei, 2001).
- Collaborative learning improves language skills by exposing learners to a variety of language inputs and requiring them to produce language output (Swain, 2000).
- Collaborative learning allows learners to develop higher-order thinking skills and construct knowledge together through shared experiences (Vygotsky, 1978).
- Collaborative learning increases cultural awareness by encouraging learners to interact with people from diverse backgrounds (Byram, 1997).

In summary, the collaborative activities presented in this chapter can significantly contribute to the language development, motivation, cognitive growth and cultural competence of ESL/EFL learners using mobile microlearning platforms. By incorporating these activities into your teaching strategies, you can create a more engaging and effective learning experience for your learners.

4.6 Design Considerations

1. How can you use diverse listening activities (e.g. podcasts, audio clips) to enhance your learners' pronunciation, comprehension, and critical thinking skills?
2. How can you design and incorporate authentic speaking activities to help your learners improve pronunciation, fluency, and confidence?
3. How can you incorporate diverse writing activities and genres to promote metacognitive awareness, coherent expression, and effective communication?
4. How can you select and incorporate diverse, engaging reading materials to enhance learners' vocabulary, comprehension, cognitive skills, and motivation?
5. How can you integrate collaborative activities in mobile microlearning to promote social interaction, motivation, and language development?

4.7 Conclusion

In this chapter, we presented a variety of mobile device-based activities to improve ESL/EFL learners listening, speaking, writing and reading skills, as well as their collaborative learning abilities. By providing learners with opportunities to interact with authentic materials, such as podcasts, audio clips, and curated playlists, teachers foster language development, boost learner confidence, and enable communication and social connections. Writing and reading exercises expose students to various genres, facilitate feedback, and enhance language proficiency, while mobile microlearning platforms provide engaging and motivating learning experiences.

References

Bond, C. D. (2012). An overview of best practices to teach listening skills. *International Journal of Listening, 26*(2), 61–63. https://doi.org/10.1080/10904018.2012.677660

Brown, G. (2017). *Listening to spoken English*. Routledge.

Byram, M. (1997). *Teaching and Assessing Intercultural Communicative Competence*. Clevedon, UK: Multilingual Matters.

Canale, M., & Swain, M. (1980). Theoretical bases of communicative approaches to second language teaching and testing. *Applied Linguistics, 1*(1), 1–47.

Celce-Murcia, M., Brinton, D. M., & Goodwin, J. M. (2010). *Teaching pronunciation: A course book and reference guide*. Cambridge University Press.

Day, R. R., & Bamford, J. (1998). *Extensive reading in the second language classroom*. Cambridge University Press.

Derwing, T. M., & Munro, M. J. (2005). Second language accent and pronunciation teaching: A research-based approach. *TESOL Quarterly, 39*(3), 379–397.

Dörnyei, Z. (2001). *Motivational Strategies in the Language Classroom*. Cambridge: Cambridge University Press. https://doi.org/10.1017/CBO9780511667343

Dörnyei, Z., & Murphy, T. (2003). *Group dynamics in the language classroom*. Cambridge University Press.

Goh, C. C. M., & Vandergrift, L. (2022). *Teaching and learning second language listening: Metacognition in action*. Routledge.

Grabe, W. (2009). *Reading in a second language: Moving from theory to practice*. Cambridge University Press.

Grabe, W., & Kaplan, R. B. (2014). *Theory and practice of writing: An applied linguistic perspective*. Routledge.

Hinkel, E. (2001). Matters of cohesion in L2 academic text. *Applied Language Learning, 12*(2), 111–132.

Hyland, F., & Hyland, K. (2006). Feedback on second language students' writing. *Language Teaching, 39*(2), 83–101.

Hyland, K. (2003). *Second language writing*. Cambridge University Press.

Jarvis, A., Kohnke, L., & Guan, G. (2020). Academic listening strategy use at an English-medium university. *The ASIAN ESP Journal, 16*(3), 8–29.

Krashen, S. (1982). *Principles and practice in second language acquisition*. Pergamon Press.

Long, M. H. (1996). The role of the linguistic environment in second language acquisition. In W. C. Ritchie & T. K. Bhatia (Eds.), *Handbook of second language acquisition* (pp. 413–468). Academic Press.

Lyster, R., & Ranta, L. (1997). Corrective feedback and learner uptake: Negotiation of form in the communicative classroom. *Studies in Second Language Acquisition, 19*(1), 37–66.

MacIntyre, P. D., & Gardner, R. C. (1991). Investigating language class anxiety using the focused essay technique. *The Modern English Language Journal, 75*(3), 296–304.

Nation, I. S. P. (2001). *Learning vocabulary in another language*. Cambridge University Press.

Nuttall, C. (2005). *Teaching reading skills in a foreign language*. Macmillan Education.

Paltridge, B. (2004). *Genre and the language learning classroom*. University of Michigan Press.

Swain, M. (1995). Three functions of output in second language learning. In G. Cook, & B. Seidlhofer (Eds.), *Principle and practice of applied linguistics: Studies in honour of H.G. Widdowson* (pp. 125–144). Oxford University Press.

Swain, M. (2000). The Output Hypothesis and beyond: Mediating Acquisition through Collaborative Dialogue. In J. P. Lantolf (Ed.), *Sociocultural Theory and Second Language Learning* (pp. 97–114). Oxford: Oxford University Press.

Taguchi, I., Gorsuch, G., & Sasamoto, E. (2006). Developing reading fluency in EFL: How assisted repeated and extensive reading affects fluency development. *Reading in a Foreign Language, 18*(1), 1–18.

Vygotsky, L. S. (1978). *Mind in Society: The Development of Higher Psychological Processes.* Cambridge, MA: Harvard University Press.

Chapter 5
Designing Microlearning Activities with Podcasts, Videos, Infographics, and Flashcards, and Microlearning Activities

Abstract This chapter examines four microlearning methods: podcasts, videos, infographics, and flashcards. While traditional classroom learning does not always accommodate students' schedules, these four methods deliver learning material in small, easily-digestible chunks. In addition, the chapter provides example activities that can be tailored to various contexts.

Keywords Podcasts · Videos · Infographics · Flashcards · Activities

5.1 Podcasts

The podcast is a useful medium for learning English and one that can be used to facilitate microlearning. Podcast hosts give lectures or hold discussions, covering subjects such as current affairs, entertainment, or breaking news. Therefore, students can select topics that fit their interests and pastimes, making studying more motivating and entertaining (Drew, 2017). Podcasts also expose learners to authentic, natural language and permit them to pause, rewind, and replay the content. In addition, the range of vocabulary and grammatical constructions in podcasts can expand learners' knowledge of and proficiency in English (Díez & Richters, 2020). Finally, listening to podcasts may improve learners' comprehension of accents and dialects (Ducate & Lomicka, 2009), allowing them to understand English speakers from different geographical areas and backgrounds (Yeh & Heng, 2022).

5.1.1 Podcast Platforms and Interactive Questions

Integrating microlearning activities into podcasts can engage learners and reinforce learning objectives. If the podcast is long, the teacher must identify the key learning objectives and separate it into bite-sized chunks. Listening to the podcast and completing the activities should take no more than six minutes. The activities developed should reinforce the key learning objective of the episode. Quizzes, reflection questions, case studies, and exercises allow learners to apply the concepts they have acquired. For example, one can incorporate quiz questions into an episode and require learners to pause the episode to answer them. Other options are to ask learners to reflect on how they could apply the concept to their studies, personal lives, or workplaces, or how they would handle a situation presented in the episode. These activities help reinforce key concepts, deepen learners' understanding of the topic, and make it more relevant to their experiences.

Depending on your requirements, financial situation, and ability to develop interactive podcast content, there are various podcast-hosting sites to choose from. The following tools and resources can be used to create interactive podcasts:

- Podbean (https://www.podbean.com/) is a podcast-hosting platform that allows you to include various interactive features in your episodes, including polls, surveys, and discussion questions. Podbean can also be integrated with third-party payment services such as Patreon and PayPal, allowing you to monetize your podcasts.
- Soundwise (https://www.soundwise.co.uk/) is a podcast-hosting platform that allows you to include quizzes, polls, calls to action, and other interactive features in your episodes.
- Anchor (https://anchor.fm/) is a podcast-hosting platform that allows you to include interactive features such as voice messages, listener feedback, and call-ins. Anchor also offers a range of editing tools and distribution options, making it an excellent choice for beginners.

The following two platforms offer limited opportunities for developing interactive content but can be used to host podcasts:

- Libsyn (https://libsyn.com/) is a well-established and widely-used podcast-hosting platform. It provides plans that range from basic to advanced and features such as analytics, social media sharing, and monetization. New users get a 14-day free trial.
- Buzzsprout (https://www.buzzsprout.com/) is an easy-to-use podcast-hosting platform with various plans, including a free program for beginners. It has detailed analytics, customizable podcast players, and integration with other tools like WordPress and YouTube. New users get a 90-day free trial.

HP5 (https://h5p.org/) is a free, open-source tool that can be used to create interactive content for podcasts, such as quizzes, games, and videos. The content can be embedded in podcast episodes, making it easy for listeners to engage with it.

These are just a few of the resources and tools available for creating interactive podcast content. There are numerous other options to consider, depending on your needs and budget. Instead of creating podcasts from scratch, teachers can also use free podcasts and resources for ESL/EFL learners available on the internet. Some possibilities include:

- **6 min English from the BBC** (https://www.bbc.co.uk/learningenglish/english/features/6-minute-english) discusses interesting topics and introduces new vocabulary in a short-form format.
- **Luke's English Podcast** (https://teacherluke.co.uk/) covers a wide range of topics, including vocabulary, grammar, and British culture.
- **Voice of America—Learning English** (https://learningenglish.voanews.com/) is a news-based podcast that helps learners improve their vocabulary and understanding of American English.

5.1.2   Sample Activity 1—Podcast

Title: Listening Comprehension: VOA News Report
Objective: To improve listening comprehension skills and learn new vocabulary.
Level: Intermediate
Duration: 6 min
Materials: Voice of America—Learning English website or their YouTube channel

Preparation:

1. Selects a VOA News Report with a suitable topic for intermediate learners.

Learner Practice:

1. Minute 1: Preparation
   Listen to the first 30 s to familiarize yourself with the topic and the speaker's voice. Grab a pen and paper to take notes.
2. Minutes 2–3: Active Listening
   Listen to the first 2 min without pausing. Focus on understanding the main ideas and take notes on any new vocabulary.
3. Minute 4: Reflection and Vocabulary
   Pause the news report and spend a minute reflecting on what you have heard. Write down the main ideas of the report. Look at the new vocabulary

words that you wrote down. Try to guess the meaning of each word from the context. Use a dictionary to check your guesses and write down the correct definitions.

4. Minute 5: Focused Listening

    Listen to the 2-min segment of the news report again. Pay close attention to the new vocabulary. Take notes on how the new words are used in context and try to understand the overall meaning of the sentences they appear in.

5. Minute 6: Wrap-up

    Review your notes and make sure you understand the main ideas. Practise the new vocabulary by making up sentences or using the words in conversation with peers.

5.1.3   Sample Activity 2—Podcast

Title: Exploring Vocabulary with 6 min English
Objective: To improve listening comprehension and vocabulary skills
Level: Elementary
Duration: 8 min
Materials: BBC Learning English Website or their YouTube Channel

Preparation:

1. Select a BBC Learning English episode with a suitable topic for elementary learners.

Learner Practice:

1. *Pre-listening (1 min):*
    Introduce the topic and pre-teach essential vocabulary.
2. *Listening (6 min):*
    Learners listen to the episode and pay close attention to the vocabulary and expressions mentioned during the episode.
3. *Post-listening (1 min):*

Ask learners to share one new vocabulary word or expression they learned. This can be done in pairs and or on Padlet allowing learners to practice speaking and reinforce their newly acquired vocabulary.

This activity provides learners with a focused and engaging way to practice listening comprehension and vocabulary skills.

5.2 Videos

We are living in an era of online videos. YouTube, TikTok, Snapchat, and Instagram offer videos that are easy to access and share. Teachers can also make videos for our students. For example, a teacher could use a mobile phone camera to make a short video about a phrasal verb to contextualize it for the learners. Such videos can be used in microlearning as stand-alone learning resources or introductory teasers that preview key learning elements. The keys to optimizing videos for microlearning are to make them engaging and immersive and to support learners as they complete the follow-up tasks. According to Köster (2018), students find videos more interesting than podcasts, PowerPoint presentations, or infographics. Videos also enhance recall and retention (Pujadas & Muñoz, 2019), which improves learning (van Alten et al., 2020). Videos can be used to provide high-impact, just-in-time lessons, such as step-by-step instructions on how to change a tire, put on safety gear, or hone customer service skills. Learners can pause and re-watch videos multiple times to improve their understanding. When making a video, it is essential to keep the content focused and let the visuals tell the story.

Several types of videos are particularly effective for English language learners:

- Instructional videos, such as tutorials or how-to guides, can provide clear and concise instructions related to specific tasks or skills. They help broaden students' vocabulary and improve their comprehension.
- Conversational videos that can be paused and allow learners to speak, such as role-playing scenarios or mock interviews, can help learners speaking and listening skills in realistic and engaging ways.
- Authentic videos, such as news clips, documentaries, or interviews, can expose learners to real-life situations and help them develop their listening and comprehension skills.

The effectiveness of videos is determined by their quality, content, and relevance to the needs and interests of the learners. Therefore, it is critical to select videos that are appropriate for the learners' levels, cultural backgrounds, and learning objectives. The teacher must also provide guidance and support to ensure that learners get as much out of the videos as possible. Additional resources and quizzes can be included to reinforce learning.

5.2.1   Video Platforms and Interactive Questions

There are many free video-making and editing apps available, including Magisto Video Editor and Creator for Android and IMotion HD for Apple IOS. Microsoft and Apple also provide video-editing tools in their software suites.

EdPuzzle (https://edpuzzle.com/) is a free platform that allows teachers to create interactive video lessons. Videos can be uploaded or imported from YouTube, Khan Academy, or other sources. Then, you can add interactive elements such as quizzes with multiple-choice, true-or-false, or open-ended questions to engage students and assess their understanding. EdPuzzle also allows teachers to track learners' performance.

The following are some examples of microlearning activities that employ various types of videos (e.g. short clips, TED Talks, news segments) and can be tailored to the needs and levels of your English language learners:

- **Fill-in-the-blank**: At regular intervals, pause the video and ask students to fill in missing words or phrases. This activity improves students' listening and vocabulary skills.
- **True/false questions**: After pausing the video, have students answer true/false questions about the content they just watched. This activity also improves their listening and comprehension abilities.
- **Multiple-choice questions**: Ask students to pause the video and select the correct answer from a list of options. This activity hones students' listening and critical thinking abilities.
- **Pronunciation practice**: Pause the video and have students repeat the words or phrases they just heard, paying particular attention to pronunciation and intonation. This activity improves students' speaking and pronunciation abilities.
- **Summary writing**: After watching the video, ask students to summarize the main points discussed. This activity improves their writing and comprehension abilities.
- **Vocabulary matching**: Stop the video and have students match new vocabulary words to their definitions. This activity expands students' vocabulary knowledge.

By using some of these activities, you can assess your students' learning while offering them engaging and effective learning experiences.

5.2.2 Sample Activity 1—Videos

Title: How to Introduce Yourself in English
Objective: To help English language learners improve their speaking and pronunciation skills when introducing themselves
Level: Any
Duration: 2 min
Materials: Video (YouTube, EdPuzzle)

Video Content:

- An introduction to the topic, including why it is important to introduce yourself in English.
- A short dialogue between two people who are introducing themselves, with subtitles to help learners follow along.
- A breakdown of key phrases and vocabulary used in the dialogue, with examples and explanations.
- A pronunciation exercise, in which learners are prompted to repeat the phrases and get feedback on their pronunciation.
- A summary of the main points covered in the video, along with suggestions for further practice.

Microlearning Activities:

- Pause the video and ask learners to repeat the phrases they just heard to practise pronunciation.
- Ask learners to write down key phrases and vocabulary used in the dialogue and use them to introduce themselves to a partner.
- Pause the video and ask learners to answer multiple-choice questions about the content they just watched.

This activity provides learners with targeted practice and feedback, helping them improve their English speaking and pronunciation skills.

5.2.3   Sample Activity 2—Videos

Title: Simple Present Tense in English
Objective: To help English language learners understand and use the simple present tense
Level: Elementary
Duration: 3 min
Materials: Video (YouTube, EdPuzzle)

Video Content: An introduction to the simple present tense; students learn when it is used and how it is formed.

- Examples of affirmative, negative, and interrogative sentences in the simple present tense, with clear explanations and visual cues.
- A breakdown of irregular verbs in the simple present tense, with examples and explanations.
- A summary of the main points covered in the video, along with suggestions for further practice.

Microlearning Activities:

- Pause the video and ask learners to identify the correct form of a verb in the simple present tense.
- Ask learners to create sentences using the simple present tense and share them with a partner.
- Pause the video and ask learners to answer a true/false question about the content.

This activity provides learners with a clear and concise explanation of the simple present tense and targeted practice activities to reinforce their understanding and facilitate retention.

Microlearning videos can be a versatile tool for enhancing learning and engagement in the classroom. They can be used as pre-class activities in flipped classrooms, as well as for self-paced learning, assessment and/or reinforcement to offer guidance and clarify misconceptions.

5.3 Infographics

Using infographics in microlearning activities is a highly effective way to engage learners who use mobile devices. Infographics are visually appealing and can be used to simplify complex information by organizing it into an easy-to-read visual format for quick reference. They provide brief overviews of new information (e.g. step-by-step instructions, timelines; Kohnke & Jarvis 2022) or serve as reminders. For infographics to be memorable, learners must be able to grasp them intuitively. Consequently, the focus should be on visual components such as charges, graphs, and colours, with minimal supplementary text. These strategies allow an infographic to communicate important content effectively (Kohnke & Chan, 2019) and learners to extract information from the images and text.

Using infographics helps cement knowledge and makes the learning process more interesting and enjoyable. To achieve these goals, the following ideas should be kept in mind when creating infographics for mobile microlearning:

- **Simplify the content**: Break down linguistic concepts into easily digestible pieces. Concentrate on a single subject or concept, such as an ordinary verb, idiomatic expression, or pronunciation guideline.
- **Use clear, bold visuals**: Employ images, graphs, and icons to present the information in an aesthetically pleasing way.
- **Limit text**: Minimize the amount of text to reduce cognitive load. Use straight-forward, plain language and concentrate on key points.
- **Organize information**: Utilize a logical layout and flow to make it easy to follow the content and understand the relationships between the various elements.
- **Optimize for mobile**: Ensure that the text is legible on small screens and that the images load rapidly.
- **Provide context**: Offer real-life examples and scenarios to help learners compre-hend how language concepts connect to real-world circumstances.
- **Include audio**: Integrate listening components to assist learners with pronuncia-tion and comprehension.
- **Incorporate interactivity**: Use components that learners can engage with, such as quizzes and clickable buttons that reveal information.
- **Use various formats**: Include timelines, flowcharts, mind maps, or comparison charts.
- **Offer supplementary resources**: Provide links to additional resources, such as video lessons, podcasts, or articles.

If you follow these suggestions, your infographics will help English language learners to improve their language skills and accelerate their learning.

5.3.1 Infographic Platforms and Interactive Questions

There are several platforms that allow one to create interactive infographics. Canva, (https://www.canva.com/), Piktochart (https://piktochart.com/), and Venngage (https://venngage.com/) are easy to use. They come with hundreds of templates that are easily modifiable, include drag-and-drop functionality, and permit simple design elements. In addition to including image carousels, pop-up texts, clickable elements, and quizzes, which can be embedded easily, these platforms make it possible to monitor learners' engagement and learning processes. The infographics produced can also be exported in either JPEG or PNG formats, making them easy to share and promote on social media platforms and in online communities.

The following are some examples of microlearning activities using infographics that can be adapted for learners of different proficiency levels, interests, and needs, making them effective ways to support language learning:

- **Vocabulary matching**: Provide a list of target vocabulary on one side of an infographic and the translations or definitions of the words on the other side. Ask learners to match each word to its translation or definition.
- **Phrasal verbs**: Create an infographic focusing on common phrasal verbs or idiomatic expressions in English. Include examples and illustrations of each phrasal verb or expression in context; then, ask learners to match them with their meanings.
- **Pronunciation practice**: Create an infographic highlighting common pronunciation issues in the English language, such as minimal pairs or consonant clusters. Include audio clips of the proper pronunciation and instruct students to listen and repeat.
- **Grammar activities**: Present grammar rules or patterns visually and include fill-in-the-blank or multiple-choice questions to help students practise these concepts.
- **Listening comprehension**: Embed short audio clips or videos that feature the target language in various contexts. After listening to each clip, learners can test their listening comprehension by answering multiple-choice or true/false questions.

5.3.2 Sample Activity 1—Infographics

Title: Ordering Food at a Restaurant
Objective: To help ESL/EFL learners practice common phrases and vocabulary used when ordering food at a restaurant
Level: Beginner
Duration: 5 min
Materials: N/A

Introduction (1 min)

1. Email learners a link to the infographic.
2. Learners read a brief introduction explaining the lesson's objective.

Activity 1: Vocabulary Matching (1.5 min)

1. Students see a list of vocabulary words related to ordering food and their definitions on the infographic. They connect the words and definitions using lines or arrows.
2. Students are instructed to take a screenshot or save the image for future reference.

Activity 2: Fill-in-the-Blank Dialogue (2 min)

1. The next section of the infographic shows a short dialogue between a customer and a waiter, with some words missing:
   Customer: Excuse me, I'd like to _____ (1) an order, please.
   Waiter: Of course! What would you like for your _____ (2)?
   Customer: I'll have the spaghetti with meatballs.
   Waiter: Anything else? Maybe an _____ (3) or a _____ (4)?
   Customer: No, thank you. Just the main course, please.
2. Students are instructed to fill in the blanks mentally using the vocabulary from the previous activity.

Conclusion (0.5 min)

1. The final section summarizes the phrases and vocabulary learnt in the lesson.
2. Students are encouraged to practise these phrases with a partner, family member, or friend to build confidence in real-life situations.

5.3.3   Sample Activity 2—Infographics

Title: Navigating Public Transportation
Objective: To introduce basic transportation vocabulary and encourage ESL/EFL learners to use it in simple sentences
Level: Elementary
Duration: 5 min
Materials: Infographic (Canva.com, Wizer.me)

Introduction: (1 min)

1. Email learners a link to the infographic.
2. Learners read a brief introduction explaining the lesson's objective.

Activity 1: Transportation Vocabulary (1.5 min)

1. On the infographic, students see colourful illustrations of modes of transportation, such as bicycles, cars, buses, trains, boats, and aeroplanes.
2. Each illustration is accompanied by the corresponding vocabulary word, written in a large, easy-to-read font.

Activity 2: Simple Sentences (2 min)

1. The next section of the infographic presents simple sentences using the transportation vocabulary, such as

   - I ride my bicycle to school.
   - My dad drives a car to work.
   - We take the bus to the park.
   - The train goes very slowly.
   - We saw a boat on the river.
   - Aeroplanes can fly high in the sky.

2. A small illustration or icon accompanies each sentence to help students understand the words in context.
3. Students are instructed to practise reading these sentences aloud.

Conclusion (0.5 min)

1. The final section summarizes the transportation vocabulary and simple sentences in the lesson.
2. Students are encouraged to practise these phrases with a partner, family member, or friend to build confidence in real-life situations.

Canva, Piktochart, and Venngage can be used to create such activities, which learners can access and complete at their own pace and on their own devices. They can then refer back to the infographics for future practice. This makes it an interesting and convenient way to practice English.

5.4 Flashcards

Interactive flashcards can be used in microlearning to introduce or review key concepts and terminology. They are easy to produce and use and can be accessed using mobile devices. Learners are engaged with the content and learn quickly when they use flashcards (Nakata, 2019; Yüksel et al., 2022). There are many benefits to using flashcards for ESL/EFL learners in mobile microlearning lessons:

- Allow learners to practice vocabulary and key phrases easily.
- Facilitate active recall.
- Provide immediate feedback.
- Can be customized for learners with different needs.
- Can be gamified.
- Enable spaced repetition.

Flashcards allow learners to actively engage with the content, leading to better memorization and instant feedback, which promotes long-term retention. In addition, the teacher can easily adjust the difficulty level as needed.

5.4.1 Flashcard Platforms and Interactive Questions

Digital flashcards are easy to create and include animations, sounds, and images. One side of each flashcard contains a keyword, phrase, number, or image, while the other side features explanatory text or animation. This method helps learners make visual connections between facts or processes and allows them to self-assess their knowledge of the subject matter. The following four flashcard sites are intuitive and include a range of functions that can be used toto create interactive flashcards.

- Anki (https://apps.ankiweb.net) is customizable, syncs between devices, and includes a free library of add-ons, including text-to-speech and cloze deletion cards.
- Memrise (https://www.memrise.com/) uses daily goals, spaced repetition, and speech recognition software to help learners practise pronunciation.
- Quizlet (https://quizlet.com/) provides game-like activities, including matching exercises, and real-time quizzes.
- Brainscape (https://www.brainscape.com/) allows for personalized learning and keeps track of the learner's responses to determine which cards are the most challenging.

The following list provides ideas and examples of microlearning flashcard exercises to use with ESL/EFL learners.

- **Vocabulary flashcards**: Place words or phrases on one side and their translations on the opposite side. Add illustrations and/or examples to facilitate comprehension.
- **Verb tenses**: Display various tenses (e.g. create separate flashcards for "runs", "ran", and "running"). Provide example phrases or sentences on each card.
- **Nouns and articles**: Create flashcards containing nouns and examples of phrases or sentences that use the correct indefinite article ("a" / "an"), definite article ("the"), or no article.
- **Prepositions**: Create flashcards listing common prepositions along with examples of their usage (e.g. "in"—"in the room").
- **Pronunciation**: Create flashcards for individual letters, letter combinations, words, and phrases. Use both phonetic symbols and audio recordings.
- **Grammar rules**: Create flashcards with grammar rules, exceptions, and examples of usage. Offer example sentences or a prompt for applying the rule.

These exercises can be digitized and expanded to include video, audio, and graphics by utilizing the aforementioned flashcard websites for flashcards. The expanded activities can also include quizzes with multiple-choice, true/false, or short-answer questions. In addition, some of the flashcard websites provide reports and statistics that evaluate students' progress and whether they need to review certain lessons.

5.4.2 Sample Activity 1—Flashcards

Title: Vocabulary Learning in a Flash
Objective: To help ESL/EFL learners expand their vocabulary and improve their language skills
Level: Beginner/intermediate
Duration: 6 min
Materials: Mobile device, digital flashcard app (e.g. Anki, Memrise, Quizlet, Brainscape), access to short videos related to the lesson content (e.g. YouTube videos) and an online quiz platform (e.g. Kahoot!, Quizzes, Google Forms)

Preparation:

1. Choose a set of 3–5 words or phrases related to the topic or grammar point of the lesson.
2. Create digital flashcards that contain the following information:

   - Front: An English word or phrase
   - Back: A translation into the learner's native language, a definition or explanation in English, and a sample sentence or example of the word being used in context

Learner Practice (6 min):

1. Minute 1: Learners review the first flashcard, focusing on the definition and pronunciation.
2. Minute 2: Learners watch a short video about the first flashcard, reinforcing the context and usage of the word or phrase.
3. Minute 3: Learners review the second flashcard, focusing on the definition and pronunciation.
4. Minute 4: Learners watch a short video related to the second flashcard, reinforcing the context and usage of the word or phrase.
5. Minute 5: Learners review the two flashcards again, this time focusing on memorizing the vocabulary and grammar rules.
6. Minute 6: Learners complete a short quiz to test their understanding of the vocabulary and grammar points.

5.4.3   Sample Activity 2—Flashcards

Title: Digital Vocabulary Learning
Objective: To help ESL/EFL learners expand their vocabulary and improve their language skills
Level: Intermediate
Duration: 5 min
Materials: Mobile device, digital flashcard app (e.g. Anki, Memrise, Quizlet, Brainscape), video conferencing app (e.g. Zoom, Skype, WhatsApp)

Preparation:

1. Choose a set of 2–5 words or expressions related to a specific topic that can spark debate
   (e.g. environment, technology). Create digital flashcards containing the following information:

   - Front: An English word or expression
   - Back: A translation into the learner's native language, a definition or explanation in English, and a sample sentence or example of the usage in context

2. Pair Work: Pair learners with a partner who has similar proficiency in the language.

Learner Practice (5 min):

1. Minute 1: Learners review the first flashcard individually, focusing on the definition and pronunciation.
2. Minute 2: Partners take turns using the word or expression from the first flashcard in sentences.
3. Minute 3: Learners review the second flashcard individually, focusing on the definition and pronunciation.
4. Minute 4: Partners take turns using the word or expression from the second flashcard in sentences.
5. Minute 5: Learners quickly review all flashcards and provide each other with feedback on their pronunciation, sentence structure, and usage.

Extension Activity: When it is their turn, students can briefly debate the subject while using the target vocabulary in sentences. To conclude, they can discuss the most compelling arguments raised during their debates.

These interactive mobile microlearning lessons can help ESL/EFL learners practise and retain their language skills efficiently and engagingly. Peer debate, a component of the extension exercise, develops critical thinking and encourages participants to go beyond basic phrase patterns.

5.5 Reflection Questions

1. Which language skills—listening, speaking, reading, and writing—do you wish to prioritize? How will the activity help your students develop those skills?
2. What level of English proficiency do your learners have? How can you tailor the content and activities to their level?
3. How will you actively engage your students (e.g. through questions, tasks, interactions, feedback)?
4. What technological tools will you use to create and deliver microlearning activities? How tech-savvy are your students? Do they have access to the necessary devices and tools?
5. How can you make the activities accessible and inclusive for learners with different needs, backgrounds, and learning styles?

5.6 Conclusion

This chapter explains how to build interactive mobile microlearning exercises using podcasts, videos, infographics, and flashcards. Podcasts offer a flexible way to learn English and a range of topics to suit personal interests. Videos are an engaging way to deliver high-impact content, while infographics present complex information in a simplified visual format. Finally, interactive flashcards can be used to introduce or review key concepts and terminology. When developing mobile microlearning activities, it is essential to employ the medium or format that is most relevant to the topic, utilize interactive content, keep activities brief, and provide feedback.

References

Díez, M. T., & Richters, M. A. (2020). Podcasting as a tool to develop speaking skills in the foreign language classroom. *EuroCALL Review, 28*(1), 40–56.

Drew, C. (2017). Edutaining audio: An exploration of education podcast design possibilities. *Educational Medial International, 54*(1), 48–62. https://doi.org/10.1080/09523987.2017.132 4360

Ducate, L., & Lomicka, L. (2009). Podcasting: An effective tool for honing language students' pronunciation? *Language Learning & Technology, 13*(3), 66–86. Retrieved from http://llt.msu. edu/vol13num3/ducatelomicka.pdf

Kohnke, L., & Chan, B. (2019). Exploiting infographics. *Modern English Teacher, 28*(1), 67–68.

Kohnke, L., & Jarvis, A. (2023). Developing infographics for English for academic purposes courses. *TESOL Journal, 14*(1), 1–5. https://doi.org/10.1002/tesj.675

Köster, J. (2018). *Video in the age of digital learning*. Springer.

Nakata, T. (2019). Learning words with flash cards and word cards. In S. Webb (Ed.), *The Routledge handbook of vocabulary studies* (pp. 304–319). Routledge.

Pujadas, G., & Muñoz, C. (2019). Extensive viewing of captioned and subtitled TV series: A study of L2 vocabulary learning by adolescents. *The Language Learning Journal, 47*(4), 479–496. https://doi.org/10.1080/09571736.2019.1616806

van Alten, D. C. D., Phielix, C., Janssen, J., & Kester, L. (2020). Self-regulated learning support in flipped learning videos enhances learning outcomes. *Computers & Education, 158*. https://doi. org/10.1016/j.compedu.2020.104000

Yeh, H. C., & Heng, L. (2022). Creating a virtual "third space" in telecollaborative project to promote English as a foreign language (EFL) learners' language proficiency and intercultural awareness. *Interactive Learning Environments*. https://doi.org/10.1080/10494820.2022.2043384

Yüksel, H. G., Mercanoğlu, H. G., & Yilmaz, M. B. (2022). Digital flashcards versus wordlist for learning technical vocabulary. *Computer Assisted Language Learning, 35*(8), 2001–2017. https://doi.org/10.1080/09588221.2020.1854312

Chapter 6
Designing Virtual Reality and Augmented Reality Microlearning Activities

Abstract Using virtual and augmented reality in the ESL/EFL classroom can create an authentic and immersive learning experience. This chapter will discuss the potential benefits of using these methods and introduce strategies, platforms, and activities that teachers can use to create learning environments that improve their learners' language proficiency.

Keywords Mobile · Microlearning · Activities · Reading · Listening · Writing · Speaking

6.1 Introduction

The previous chapter examined how to optimize mobile microlearning to help ESL/EFL students improve their language skills. This chapter focuses on creating microlearning activities that utilize virtual reality (VR) and augmented reality (AR). VR and AR can fully immerse learners in the English language and create an authentic and contextualized learning environment (Huang et al., 2021). Learners are intrinsically motivated when they are engaged in realistic scenarios and tasks (Shadiev & Yang, 2020) and the learning is tailored to their requirements, talents, and interests (Di Natale et al., 2020). Moreover, VR and AR can incorporate gamification to make learning more entertaining and efficient (Chen & Hsu, 2020). Within virtual spaces, students can complete missions, gain awards, overcome obstacles, and reach new levels.

VR and AR platforms also allow for collaboration. Students can work and learn together, even if they are in different physical locations. Through VR and AR, they can engage in natural and intuitive ways via gestures, movements, touching, and speech (Reitz et al., 2019). As many students wear smartwatches and use mobile devices, making use of these for microlearning can make the learning experience highly accessible—some AR apps only require mobile devices, not headsets—and promote independent learning.

When creating VR and AR activities for ESL/EFL learners, it is important to keep the following strategies in mind:

- **Teach cultural context**: Use immersive scenarios that allow learners to gain cultural knowledge and awareness.
- **Foster collaboration**: Have learners work together in the same virtual space to complete tasks, solve problems, create projects, and hold discussions.
- **Provide situated learning**: Place students in contextualised scenarios that simulate real-life situations and environments.
- **Incorporate gamification**: Include challenges, levels, rewards, and scores.
- **Use existing content**: Use ready-made simulations, lessons, and games, customizing them to meet the learners' needs.

6.2 Virtual Reality Platforms

Learners can use either iOS or Android to access mobile applications and platforms designed for language instruction. Some VR language learning applications are free for learners. Those listed below offer realistic and engaging opportunities to practice speaking and listening in a virtual environment:

- **VirtualSpeech** (https://virtualspeech.com/) offers a free plan and focuses on public speaking and communication skills.
- **Engage** (https://engagevr.io/) offers a free plan with restricted access to language-learning sessions focusing on speaking and listening practice.
- **AltspaceVR** (https://altvr.com/) allows learners to participate in free events and activities, including language-learning meetups and chat groups.
- **VRChat** (https://hello.vrchat.com/) permits learners to create and explore virtual worlds, engage with other users, and participate in various activities for free.

Instructors must remember that students may need a VR headset compatible with their smartphones to use some of these applications. Depending on their budget and personal preferences, learners can choose from headsets as inexpensive as Google Cardboard or as pricey as Oculus Rift.

6.2.1 Sample Activity 1—Virtual Reality

Title: Virtual Reality Immersive Conversation
Objective: To help ESL/EFL learners practice their listening and speaking skills
Level: Beginner to advanced
Duration: 5 min

Materials: AA mobile device with a VR headset (e.g. Google Cardboard, Samsung Gear VR) and a language learning app or platform that supports VR experiences (e.g. VirtualSpeech)

Preparation:

1. Choose a VR platform or language-learning app that fits the level of the learners.
2. Choose a situation for students to practise in the VR environment (e.g. going to a party or a business meeting)) or a specific language skill to focus on (e.g. asking for something, giving an opinion, negotiating).

Learner Practice (5 min):

1. *Minute 1*: Learners use their VR headsets to select the scenario.
2. *Minutes 2–4*: Learners participate in an immersive conversation with virtual characters, listening to them and responding in kind. They practise saying words, putting sentences together, and having a realistic conversation.
3. *Minute 5*: Learners leave the VR environment and reflect on their performance, writing down problems they faced, new words or phrases they learnt, and areas in which they could improve.

6.2.2 Sample Activity 2—Virtual Reality

Title: Virtual Scavenger Hunt
Objective: To improve ESL/EFL learners' listening and speaking skills and vocabulary acquisition
Level: Intermediate
Duration: 6 min
Materials: AA mobile device with the VirtualSpeech app installed

Preparation:

1. Select an environment with many objects or scenes for learners to explore.
2. Create a list of 5–7 brief audio clues related to objects or scenes in the environment.

Learner Practice:

1. *Introduction:* Explain the activity to the learners and instruct them to install the VirtualSpeech app.
2. *Starting the challenge:* Share the name of the environment and ask them to navigate to it within the app. Inform them they have only 6 min to complete the challenge.
3. *Listening to the clue:* Give the first audio clue. The clue should be concise and guide them to identify a specific object or scene (e.g. "an object used in a kitchen for cooking food on a stove").
4. *Answering questions:* When they have identified the object or scene, learners say a sentence using the word or describing the scene (e.g. "I use a frying pan to cook scrambled eggs in the morning").
5. *Proceed to the next clue:* Give the next audio clue as soon as the learners answer. Steps 3 and 4 should be repeated for each clue on the list.
6. *Wrap-up:* After 6 min, get the learners together and discuss what they did. Ask them to discuss any new words they learnt and how challenging and/ or interesting they found the activity.

Extension: Make it more competitive by keeping track of the time taken to answer each clue so learners can compare themselves with each other.

6.3 Augmented Reality Platforms

Augmented reality can make learning fun and engaging for learners while improving their language proficiency (Parmaxi & Demetriou, 2020). Teachers can create AR experiences to help learners practice vocabulary, grammar, and listening skills personalized and realistic contexts, providing 3D visualizations to help them understand concepts and engage in effective communication. For example, one can create an AR scavenger hunt or an interactive quiz that learners can access using their smartphones. Using AR in ESL/EFL instruction can also promote production, collaboration, and cultural understanding (Radu, 2014). The following list includes some common applications that can be used to develop AR activities:

- **Google Lens** (https://lens.google/) is an image recognition app that can identify objects and text in real life.
- **Wikitude** (https://www.wikitude.com/) is a platform that allows users to create and experience interactive content
- **SketchAR** (https://sketchar.io/) is a drawing app that teaches users how to draw by providing step-by-step instructions overlaid on real-world surfaces.
- **Blippar** (https://www.blippar.com/) allows users to create and experience interactive, digital content overlaid on physical objects or environments.
- **Quiver** (https://quivervision.com/) is a colouring app that brings 2D images to life. It can create interactive, 3D models of vocabulary items, scenes, or stores.
- **AR Flashcard** (https://arflashcards.com/) allows learners to scan flashcards and bring up 3D models of objects, animals, and other items.

Augmented reality gives ESL/EFL students a more immersive and interactive way to learn. By using augmented reality (AR) activities, students can take part in real-world, context-based situations that help them improve their language skills and feel more confident when communicating with people in the real world.

6.3.1 Sample Activity 1—Augmented Reality

Title: Finding and Describing Objects
Objective: To practise speaking and vocabulary skills
Level: Beginner to advanced
Duration: 5 min
Materials: A mobile device with an AR application (e.g. Google Lens, AR Flashcard) and 5–7 printed images of everyday objects

Preparation:

1. Select 5–7 objects that learners can describe using various adjectives and phrases.
2. Find or create images of these objects. Use an AR application to create an overlap or 3D model for each image.
3. Print the image with the AR trigger or QR code.
4. Place the printed images around the classroom.

Learner Practice:

1. *Introduction*: Explain the activity to the learners. Instruct them to install the AR application.
2. *Starting the activity*: Learners walk around the classroom, scan each image using the AR app, and describe the objects using at least three adjectives or phrases. Encourage learners to say their descriptions out loud or write them down for additional practice.
3. *Wrap-up*: Ask learners to share the objects they found and the descriptions they created. Review the correct usage of adjectives and phrases, and discuss any challenges or difficulties encountered during the activity.

This activity can be made more interactive by having learners work in pairs or small groups to encourage peer learning and collaboration.

6.3.2   Sample Activity 2—Augmented Reality

Title: AR Reading Quiz
Objective: To practise reading comprehension and vocabulary skills
Level: Beginner to advanced
Duration: 5 min
Materials: A mobile device with an AR application (e.g. Blippar), a short, printable text passage appropriate for learners' proficiency level, 3–4 multiple-choice questions related to the passage

Preparation:

1. Select or create a short text.
2. Prepare 3–4 multiple-choice questions and use an AR App to create an overlay.
3. Link each question to a specific part of the text.
4. Print the text passage with the AR trigger image or QR code.

Learner Practice:

1. *Introduction*: Explain the activity to the learners and instruct them to install the AR application.
2. *Starting the challenge*: Distribute the printed text passage with the AR trigger image or QR code. Inform learners that they have 4 min to complete the challenge.
3. *Reading the passage*: Learners use the AR application to scan the trigger image or QR code to reveal the text passage. They should read the passage quickly, focusing on understanding the main ideas and unfamiliar vocabulary.
4. *Answering questions*: After reading the passage, learners use the AR application to access the multiple-choice questions related to the passage.
5. *Wrap-up*: After 4 min are up, gather the learners to discuss their experiences. Ask them to share any new vocabulary they learnt and review the correct answers to the questions.

This activity can be adapted for learners of different proficiency levels by adjusting the complexity of the text passage and questions.

6.4 Potential Challenges

Various obstacles that must be overcome when using AR and VR with ESL/EFL students. These forms of technology must be incorporated with care so they do not become an unwelcome distraction or cause cognitive overload. Working with AR and VR requires a stable internet connection and special equipment, which not all students or classrooms have. Also, teachers need training to integrate AR and VR into the classroom in ways that promote student learning. Creating and executing AR and VR content requires substantial time and effort. However, by adhering to the practical principles for maximizing mobile microlearning presented in Chap. 3, instructors can address these concerns proactively.

6.5 Reflection Questions

The following questions can help you make informed decisions on how to use AR and VR technology in the classroom:

1. How can VR and AR activities be designed to engage and motivate learners, especially those less inclined to participate in traditional classroom activities?
2. How do the planned VR and AR activities align with the overall learning objectives of the ESL/EFL curriculum? What specific language skills do the activities target?
3. How can VR and AR promote learner autonomy and self-directed learning?
4. How can teachers assess the effectiveness of VR and AR activities in terms of language acquisition and skill development?

6.6 Conclusion

This chapter has highlighted ways to integrate VR and AR into ESL/EFL teaching to enhance learning and create immersive experiences. Teachers must select the platforms that fit their budget, students, and aims. The platforms and activities included in this chapter offer learners authentic and engaging opportunities to practise English in a realistic virtual environment. When integrating VR and AR, teachers need to avoid cognitive overload and ensure that they can access the necessary technological resources. They also must be trained in the use of these technologies. Effective planning and preparation will allow them to create VR and AR materials that meet their students' needs, interests, and competency levels.

References

Chen, Y. L., & Hsu, C. C. (2020). Self-regulated mobile game-based English learning in virtual reality environment.*Computers & Education, 154*.https://doi.org/10.1016/j.compedu.2020.103910

Di Natale, A. F., Repetto, C., Riva, G., & Villani, D. (2020). Immersive virtual reality in K-12 and higher education: A 10-year systematic review of empirical research. *British Journal of Educational Technology, 51*(6), 2006–2033. https://doi.org/10.1111/bjet.13030

Huang, X., Zou, D., Cheng, G., & Xie, H. (2021). A systematic review of AR and VR enhancing language learning. *Sustainability, 13*(9), 4639. https://doi.org/10.3390/su13094639

Parmaxi, A., & Demetriou, A. A. (2020). Augmented reality in language learning: A state-of-the-art review of 2014–2019. *Journal of Computer Assisted Learning, 36*(6), 861–875. https://doi.org/10.1111/jcal.12486

Radu, I. (2014). Augmented reality in education: A meta-review and cross-media analysis. *Personal and Ubiquitous Computing, 18*, 1533–1543. https://doi.org/10.1007/s00779-013-0747-y

Reitz, L., Sohny, A., & Lochmann, G. (2019). VR-based gamification of communication training and oral examination in a second language. *International Journal of Game-Based Learning, 6*(2), 46–61. https://doi.org/10.4018/IJGBL.2016040104

Shadiev, R., & Yang, M. (2020). Review of studies on technology-enhanced language learning and teaching. *Sustainability, 12,* 524. https://doi.org/10.3390/su12020524

Chapter 7
Microlearning with Chatbots

Abstract This chapter introduces and defines learning chatbots and explores the role they play in language teaching and learning. It includes microlearning activities making use of chatbots that practitioners can incorporate into their classes.

Keywords Chatbots · Microlearning · Language learning · Activities

7.1 Introduction to Chatbots

Since the launch of ChatGPT ('generative, pre-trained transformer') by OpenAI in November 2002, language teachers have begun to pay attention to such chatbots (Kohnke et al., 2023), which can simulate human-like conversations, answer questions intelligently, and tell stories (Pereira & Diaz, 2018). A chatbot is a computer application with the ability to respond to prompts and engage in discussions with a user through text and/or voice (Ashfaque et al., 2020).

Early chatbots followed a pre-defined set of rules derived from external knowledge and could only answer pre-programmed questions. They were integrated into websites and social media to provide users with information or engage in dialogues on specific topics. For example, they answered frequently asked questions and served as virtual travel agents or quiz hosts. Today, chatbots can be found in entertainment, commerce, and the public sector.

Intelligent chatbots like ChatGPT can leverage artificial intelligence (AI) techniques such as natural language processing (NLP), machine learning (ML), and deep learning (DL). They respond to questions using knowledge obtained from a vast dataset of human language (Jiang et al., 2022). What makes these AI chatbots 'intelligent' is their ability to learn from previous interactions and improve over time (Fryer et al., 2019). As language tutors, they can facilitate lessons and offer exercises to enhance learners' listening, reading, speaking, and writing. In addition, ChatGPT can explain the meaning of a word in context in multiple languages, offer dictionary definitions and sample sentences, correct and explain grammatical errors, and write paragraphs and essays. Learners can receive immediate feedback and practise the target language anytime and anywhere, using a chatbot as an on-demand conversation partner (Kim, 2017).

Despite these advantages, the emergence of ChatGPT has sparked debate among language teachers because of its ability to generate unique responses based on a single prompt and create content that seems to have been written by a human. However, it is important to note that using chatbots in language teaching is not a new phenomenon.

7.2   A Brief History of Chatbots

In 1956, the world's first chatbot, ELIZA, was developed. It used a pattern-matching and substitution methodology to facilitate 'authentic interaction' comprising text-based input and output (Weizenbaum, 1966). This gave users the illusion that the chatbot could understand them, even though it could not participate in discourse or converse intelligently; it could only follow the script with which it had been programmed. Still, ELIZA passed the Turing Test, which is used to determine whether a computer or software application can be distinguished from a human being. Many users were convinced of ELIZA's intelligence and understanding, attributing human-like feelings to the software.

Since the introduction of ELIZA, the capabilities of chatbots using text and natural language interfaces have developed rapidly. Each new chatbot attempts to simulate human interaction more accurately and thoroughly than the last (Shawar & Atwell, 2007). Inspired by ELIZA, Wallace (1990) created the world's largest open-source chatbot, ALICE (Artificial Linguistic Internet Computer Entity), which was based on natural language understanding and pattern-matching related to topics and categories. ALICE could generate intelligent responses because it contained sets of answers related to various topics and sub-topics, which were matched to the user's query. However, unlike ELIZA, it was unable to pass the Turing Test, as users often exposed flaws in its conversations. Due to its excessive reliance on a restrictive set of rules and scripts, its replies quickly became monotonous and incoherent.

Another chatbot that used textual input clues to formulate optimal answers was Cleverbot. Unlike earlier chatbots, Cleverbot 'learnt' from its conversations and used this knowledge to determine how to respond in the future (Hill et al., 2015). One of its key features was that it would analyse the whole conversation to select the best possible answer, instead of only considering the most recent question. Like ELIZA, it passed the Turing Test.

7.3 Chatbots as Facilitators of Language Learning

Chatbots continue to attract a great deal of attention because they can support the autonomy of language learners (Shawar & Atwell, 2007), act as interactive interlocutors (Chang et al., 2010), and motivate learners (Jia & Chen, 2008). The literature suggests that chatbots allow learners to (i) practise listening, (ii) study words and expressions, (iii) obtain immediate grammar and spelling feedback, and (iv) access a supportive learning environment (Fryer & Carpenter, 2006). Lee et al. (2013) noted that students' interactions and negotiation of meaning improved when they used a chatbot to engage in communicative activities, while Shim et al. (2012) found that their speaking fluency and task completion improved. Chatbots that can conduct formative assessments and provide immediate feedback have also been developed (Huang et al., 2019; Kuhail et al., 2023).

Another advantage of chatbots is that they provide an anxiety-free learning environment that is always available. Learners can practise, receive automatic error correction, and have key content repeated (Fryer & Carpenter, 2006). These features make learning tasks manageable and enjoyable (Huang et al., 2022). Additionally, chatbots decrease the perceived transactional distance (Moore, 1997) between learners and teachers (Kohnke, 2022a) and allow learners to ask questions without fear (Fryer & Carpenter, 2006). In addition, students enjoy conversing with chatbots more than with other students and teachers (Fryer et al., 2020). Finally, chatbots provide timely and relevant teaching (Kohnke, 2023).

During the school closures and suspension of face-to-face learning during the COVID-19 pandemic, chatbots began to serve as intelligent language-learning tutors (Kohnke, 2022b). For example, they provided timely reassurance and clarification related to homework and assignments, as well as a sense of interaction in what was otherwise a period of isolation. This suggests the promising ability of AI chatbots to enhance or trigger interest in language learning among ESL/EFL students.

However, chatbots also have limitations as language-learning tools. For instance, they may not stay on topic and learners must be able to spell their inquiries correctly to receive an appropriate response (Coniam, 2008; Fryer & Nakao, 2009).

7.4 Chatbot Platforms

Microlearning activities using chatbots can be an engaging and effective way to help learners acquire a language quickly and efficiently. The following three platforms can be used to create customized chatbots. They feature visual drag-and-drop interfaces, a range of templates and design elements, support quizzes, surveys, and automated responses. They can also be integrated with social media (e.g. Facebook, WhatsApp):

- BotStar (https://www.botstar.com/)
- ManyChat (https://manychat.com/)
- Chatfuel (https://chatfuel.com/)

These three platforms can help novice developers create engaging and effective mobile microlearning activities using chatbots. Alternatively, they can take advantage of existing chatbots.

7.5 Existing Chatbots

There are several chatbots that specifically designed for English language learning:

- Andy English Bot (https://andychatbot.com/), which assists learners with everyday conversations.
- Mondly (https://www.mondly.com/), which presents flashcards that help users memorize words and pronunciation.
- Duolingo (https://www.duolingo.com/) offers a speech-to-text tool that responds with contextually-appropriate answers and encourages interaction.
- Babbel (https://www.babbel.com/), which offers personalized lessons and exercises, simulates real-life conversations, and provides instant feedback for learners.
- Hello English (https://helloenglish.com/) is a chatbot specifically designed to help learners improve their English skills. It offers a range of lessons, quizzes and games that focus on vocabulary, grammar and pronunciation.

7.6 Suggested Activities for English Language Learning

Today, free chatbots that accept input and produce output can be found online. Therefore, it is possible to incorporate non-language-specific chatbots into language-learning activities. The following list provides some examples of activities that use chatbots to support English language learning:

1. **Vocabulary building**
   A chatbot can provide learners with a new English word or phrase, its definition, and an example sentence every day and ask them to practise using it in a sentence. The chatbot can then provide feedback on their response and help them improve their language skills.
2. **Grammar practice**
   A chatbot can ask learners to complete short exercises related to specific grammar points, such as verb tenses or prepositions. It can provide instant feedback on their responses and offer additional activities if needed.
3. **Writing prompts**
   A chatbot can provide learners with writing prompts or topics, helping them develop their writing skills. It can give them feedback to help them improve the style and structure of their writing.

4. **Grammar and spelling correction**
   A chatbot can provide instant feedback to help learners correct their grammar and spelling errors. This is particularly useful for learners who do not have access to a teacher or tutor.

5. **Pronunciation practice**
   A chatbot can provide learners with audio recordings of commonly mispronounced words and allow them to practise saying them correctly. It can give feedback on their pronunciation and help them improve their speaking skills.

6. **Conversational practice**
   A chatbot can simulate real-life conversations, allowing learners to practise speaking and listening in a low-pressure environment. It can provide feedback on the correct use of idioms, helping them to improve their conversational skills.

7. **Listening comprehension**
   A chatbot can provide learners with audio recordings of English conversations and ask them questions about the content. It can give feedback on their responses and help them improve their listening comprehension skills.

8. **Reading comprehension**
   A chatbot can deliver a short reading passage and ask learners to answer questions about the text. It can provide instant feedback on their responses and help them improve their reading comprehension skills.

9. **Feedback and correction**
   A chatbot can provide learners with feedback on their writing and help them to revise and improve their work. It can highlight areas in need of improvement and provide suggestions to make the writing clearer and more concise.

10. **Error correction**
    A chatbot can provide instant feedback on learners' responses and help them correct their errors in speaking and listening. This is particularly helpful for learners who do not have access to a teacher or tutor.

11. **Role-play scenarios**
    A chatbot can simulate a real-life scenario, such as ordering a coffee at a coffee shop or food at a restaurant. Learners can practise their language skills by interacting with the chatbot and receiving feedback on their responses.

12. **Quizzes**
    A chatbot can generate short quizzes to test the learner's knowledge of vocabulary, grammar, or other language skills. It can provide instant feedback on their responses, help them improve, and keep track of their progress over time.

These general activities can also be personalized based on the needs of individual learners to provide a tailor-made learning experience. Wang and Petrina (2013) note that chatbots used to promote language acquisition have three essential characteristics: (i) allow for repetition, (ii) have a matching ability to provide appropriate responses, and (iii) provide adequate feedback. While there is no specific roadmap for creating microlearning activities using chatbots, following these suggestions and guidelines will ensure that you can design and offer robust learning activities.

7.6.1   Sample Activity 1—Chatbots

Title: Conversational Practice with Chatbots
Objective: To help ESL/EFL learners practice their conversational skills and improve language fluency
Level: Beginner to intermediate
Duration: 5 min
Materials: A mobile device with access to language learning chatbots (e.g. Duolingo Chatbot, Mondly, or Replica)

Preparation:

1. Choose a chatbot app that is designed for language learning and is suitable for the learners' proficiency level.
2. Choose a topic or situation (e.g. ordering food, asking for directions, making a reservation) or a grammar point (e.g. using the past tense, making conditional sentences, using phrasal verbs) for students to practise.

Learner Practice:

1. Minute 1: Learners start a conversation with the chatbot on their mobile devices, telling it who they are and what they want to learn.
2. Minute 2: Learners ask questions or make statements about the chosen topic to practise putting together and pronouncing sentences.
3. Minute 3: Learners read or listen to the chatbot's answers, focusing on understanding and noticing any new words or structures.
4. Minute 4: Learners continue talking with the chatbot, adding in the new words or grammar structures they have learnt from the chatbot.
5. Minute 5: Learners bring the conversation to a close and think about any problems they encountered or new language skills they picked up during the session.

7.6.2 Sample Activity 2—Chatbots

Title: Chatbot Reading Comprehension Challenge
Objective: To help ESL/EFL learners practise and improve their reading skills and comprehension.
Level: Intermediate and advanced
Duration: 4 min
Materials: A mobile device with access to language learning chatbots (e.g. Duolingo Chatbot, Mondly, or Replica)

Preparation: Choose a chatbot app that is designed for language learning and is suitable for the learners' proficiency level.

Learner Practice:

1. Minute 1: Learners talk to the chatbot using their mobile devices, asking for a short text with complex sentence structures and idiomatic expressions.
2. Minute 2: Learners read the text, focusing on comprehension and identifying new words or phrases.
3. Minute 3: Learners ask the chatbot for clarification or explanations of the new words or phrases, keeping the context in mind the context.
4. Minute 4: Learners write a summary of the text or answer questions provided by the chatbot to demonstrate their comprehension.

These two exercises provide learners with a safe, low-pressure environment to improve their speaking and listening abilities. Learners should be encouraged to engage in regular practice, adjusting the content and difficulty as necessary to ensure they remain challenged and motivated.

7.7 Reflection Questions

1. What are the potential benefits of using chatbots for language learning?
2. How can chatbots support different language skills in your context, including speaking, listening, reading, and writing?
3. What are the potential drawbacks of using chatbots for language learning?

4. How can chatbots support language learning among learners of different ages
    and ability levels?
5. How can the effectiveness of chatbots be evaluated?

7.8 Conclusion

This chapter has provided a brief overview of chatbots and discussed their pedagogical strengths in terms of facilitating language acquisition among ESL/EFL learners. Teachers need to select the most appropriate chatbot to meet their pedagogical goals and be aware that chatbot responses may be redundant, predictable, and lack human personality. The activities suggested in this chapter offer a starting point for using chatbots in microlearning. When implemented effectively, chatbots can improve the overall quality of education and function as useful tools for helping learners meet their language goals.

References

Ashfaque, M. W., Tharewal, S., Iqhbal, S., & Kayte, C. N. (2020). A review on techniques, characteristics and approaches to an intelligent tutoring chatbot system. In *International Conference on Smart Innovations in Design, Environment, Management, Planning and Computing* (ICSIDEMPC) (pp. 258–262). IEEE.

Chang, C. W., Lee, J. H., Chao, P. Y., Wang, C. Y., & Chen, G. D. (2010). Exploring the possibility of using humanoid robots as instructional tools for teaching a second language in primary school. *Educational Technology and Society, 13*(2), 13–24.

Coniam, D. (2008). Evaluating the language resources of chatbots for their potential in English as a second language. *ReCALL, 20*(1), 98–116. https://doi.org/10.1017/S0958344008000815

Fryer, L. K., & Carpenter, R. (2006). Emerging technologies—Bots as language learning tools. *Language Learning and Technology, 10*(3), 8–14. 10125/44068

Fryer, L. K., & Nakao, K. (2009). Assessing chatbots for EFL use. In A. Stoke (Ed.), JALT2008 Conference Proceedings. Tokyo: JALT. http://jalt-publications.org/proceedings/articles/84-jalt2009-proceedings-contents

Fryer, L. K., Coniam, D., Carpenter. R., & Lăpușneanu, D. (2020). Bots for language learning now: Current and future directions. *Language Learning & Technology, 24*(2), 8–22. Retrieved from http://hdl.handle.net/10125/44719

Fryer, L. K., Nakao, K., & Thompson, A. (2019). Chatbot learning partners: Connecting learning experiences, interest and competence. *Computers in Human Behavior, 93*, 279–289. https://doi.org/10.1016/j.chb.2018.12.023

Hill, J., Ford, W. R., & Farreres, I. G. (2015). Real conversations with artificial intelligence: A comparison between human-human online conversations and human-chatbot conversations. *Computers in Human Behavior, 49*, 245–250. https://doi.org/10.1016/j.chb.2015.02.026

Huang, W., Hew, K. F., & Fryer, L. K. (2022). Chatbots for language learning—Are they really useful? A systematic review of chatbot-supported language learning. *Journal of Computer Assisted Learning, 38*(1), 237–257. https://doi.org/10.1111/jcal.12610

Huang, W., Hew, K. F., & Gonda, D. E. (2019). Designing and evaluating three chatbot-enhanced activities for a flipped graduate course. *International Journal of Mechanical Engineering and Robotics Research, 8*(5), 813–818. https://doi.org/10.18178/ijmerr.8.5.813-818

Jia, J., & Chen, W. (2008). Motivate the learners to practice English through playing with chatbot CSIEC. In: Z. Pan, X. Zhang, A. El Rhalibi, W. Woo, & Y. Li (Eds.), *Technologies for E-learning and digital entertainment. Edutainment 2008. Lecture notes in computer science* (vol. 5093). Springer. https://doi.org/10.1007/978-3-540-69736-7_20

Jiang, H., Cheng, Y., Yang, J., & Gao, S. (2022). AI-powered chatbot communication with customers: Dialogic interactions, satisfaction, engagement, and customer behavior. *Computers in Human Behavior, 134*, 107329. https://doi.org/10.1016/j.chb.2022.107329

Kim, N.-Y. (2017). Effects of different types of text-based chat on Korean EFL students' writing performance. *Korean Journal of Linguistics, 42*(3), 277–301.

Kohnke, L. (2023). L2 learners' perception of a chatbot as a potential independent language learning tool. *International Journal of Mobile Learning and Organisation, 17*(1/2), 214–226. https://doi.org/10.1504/IJMLO.2023.10053355

Kohnke, L. (2022a). A qualitative exploration of student perspectives of chatbot use during emergency remote teaching. *International Journal of Mobile Learning and Organisation, 16*(4), 475–488. https://doi.org/10.1504/IJMLO.2022.125966

Kohnke, L. (2022b). A pedagogical chatbot: A supplemental language learning tools. *RELC Journal*, (OnlineFirst). https://doi.org/10.1177/00336882211067054

Kohnke, L., Moorhouse, B. L., & Zou, D. (2023). Using chat GPT for language teaching and learning. *RELC Journal*. https://doi.org/10.1177/00336882231162868

Kuhail, M. A., Alturki, N., Alramlawi, S., & Alhejori, K. (2023). Interacting with educational chatbots: A systematic review. *Education and Information Technologies, 28*, 973–1018. https://doi.org/10.1007/s10639-022-11177-3

Lee, S., Min, D., & Shim, G. (2013). Effects of using an educational robot on interactional aspects in group-based communicative activities. *Journal of the Korea English Education Society, 12*(2), 61–80.

Moore, M. (1997). Theory of transactional distance. In D. Keegan (Ed.), *Theoretical principles of distance education* (pp. 22–38). Routledge.

Pereira, J., & Díaz, Ó. (2018). Chatbot dimensions that matter: Lessons from the trenches', In T. Mikkonen, R. Klamma, & J. Hernández (Eds.), *Web Engineering. International Conference on Web Engineering* (pp. 129–135). Springer. https://doi.org/10.1007/978-3-319-91662-0_9

Shawar, B. A., & Atwell, E. (2007). Fostering language learner autonomy through adaptive conversation tutors. *Paper presented at the Proceedings of the 4th Corpus Linguistics Conference* (pp. 1–9), Birmingham, UK.

Shim, K. N., Min, D.-G., & Lee, S. (2012). A model of robot-assisted assessment of primary school students' English speaking. *The Korea Association of Primary English Education, 18*(3), 399–417.

Wallace, R. S. (1990). The anatomy of A.L.I.C.E. Retrieved from https://freeshell.de/~chali/programowanie/Anatomy_of_ALICE.pdf

Wang, Y. F., & Petrina, S. (2013). Using learning analytics to understand the design of an intelligent language tutor–chatbot lucy. *Editorial Preface, 4*(11), 124–131.

Weizenbaum, J. (1966). ELIZA—A computer program for the study of natural language communication between man and machine. *Communications of the ACM, 9*(1), 36–45.

Chapter 8
Microlearning in the Education of the Future

Abstract This chapter concludes the book by concisely addressing the limitations of microlearning and suggesting directions for future research and practice. It highlights the need for a comprehensive understanding of microlearning's potential drawbacks and challenges in order to optimise its use in ESL/EFL education. The chapter culminates with seven practical guidelines for designing effective mobile microlearning activities tailored to ESL/EFL students. These guidelines emphasize the importance of addressing individual learner needs, fostering engagement, and promoting collaboration to create a rich and meaningful learning experience. By following these recommendations, teachers can harness the power of mobile microlearning and create a supportive, dynamic environment that maximise language learning outcomes for their students.

Keywords Microlearning · Limitations · Future research · Practice · Guidelines

8.1 Introduction

Mobile microlearning has become a popular approach that allows ESL/EFL learners to enhance their language skills. With the ubiquity of mobile devices, learners can access language learning anytime and anywhere. Moreover, because the content is delivered in bite-sized chunks and users can revisit it repeatedly using their mobile devices (Lee, 2021), the retention rate is greater than that of conventional learning methods (Mohammed et al., 2018). Gamification, interactive multimedia, and social learning features also make mobile microlearning more engaging and effective (Dolasinski & Reynolds, 2021; Epp & Phirangee, 2019). As artificial intelligence, machine learning, and natural language processing advance, mobile applications will be able to analyse learners' strengths and weaknesses and offer personalized feedback and recommendations. This will help learners focus on areas they need to practise and improve their language skills effectively. These applications will also be able to adapt to individual learning styles and preferences.

Additionally, we can anticipate the greater integration of virtual and augmented reality features into mobile microlearning. This will offer learners immersive and

© The Author(s), under exclusive license to Springer Nature Singapore Pte Ltd. 2023   81
L. Kohnke, *Using Technology to Design ESL/EFL Microlearning Activities*,
SpringerBriefs in Education, https://doi.org/10.1007/978-981-99-2774-6_8

interactive language learning experiences, enabling them to practise real-life conversations. Overall, the future of mobile microlearning for ESL/EFL learners appears promising: it will include more personalized, adaptive approaches and the integration of new technologies that will enrich the learning experience.

8.2   Limitations

While mobile microlearning can be effective for ESL/EFL learners, it does have some potential drawbacks. It may not provide the same level of interaction and engagement as in-person classes, causing learners who require more structured support to struggle. Teachers could integrate mobile microlearning with in-class activities and encourage learners to participate in conversation clubs. Although mobile microlearning activities should provide instant feedback, this feedback may not be as comprehensive as what a teacher can provide. Thus, teachers must consider these limitations and supplement mobile learning with other forms of learning when it is feasible. Teachers should also keep in mind that not all learners may have access to mobile devices, creating a digital divide that could limit the effectiveness of mobile microlearning. To address this limitation, teachers can explore incorporating mobile microlearning activities into computer lab sessions. Finally, it can be challenging to monitor learners' progress and hold them accountable when using mobile microlearning tools. It is suggested that teachers set clear expectations and regularly review learner's progress.

Microlearning provides numerous benefits and opportunities for ESL/EFL learners, but it is essential to address any implementation challenges that may arise. Teachers can create engaging and effective language learning experiences for their students by selecting and curating resources with care, establishing clear expectations, and integrating mobile microlearning with traditional teaching methods and face-to-face interaction.

8.3   Directions for Future Research and Practice

This book aims to guide language teachers in developing microlearning activities by introducing the concept of mobile microlearning and offering strategies, tools, and best practices for incorporating it into ESL/EFL instruction. Given the rapid pace of technological growth, creating future-proof guidelines is challenging. Therefore, engaging in action research, which is widely employed in education (see Burns et al., 2022), can help us understand approaches that work locally and those that can be shared across contexts (Baumfield et al., 2013). Teachers may find the action–reflection cycle (McNiff & Whitehead, 2011) a particularly suitable starting point: (1) investigate a teaching-related problem or question; (2) research and reflect on it; (3) take action to improve one's teaching; (4) evaluate the effectiveness of this action; (5) extend or modify the initial action; (6) disseminate the results.

8.4 Concluding Thoughts

Integrating microlearning into traditional courses may initially seem daunting. However, targeted microlessons that leverage emerging technologies can be created and delivered using the information in this book as a starting point and guide. By optimizing materials for mobile learning, it is possible to ensure that learners can fit it into their busy schedules and access it anytime and anywhere. The concise, engaging, and interactive content delivery method used in microlearning aligns with the information-gathering style and needs of the current generation (Donahue, 2016; Winger, 2018). They prefer six-minute multimodal activities focusing on bite-sized chunks of content over reading lengthy sections of traditional textbooks.

As you embark on designing and optimizing microlearning activities for mobile devices, the following seven tips can help:

1	Make it focused	Centre each activity on one learning objective
2	Make it simple	Ensure that the text and layout are easy to follow
3	Make it graphic	Use visuals to illustrate the topic
4	Make it interactive	Keep the activities engaging to increase levels of motivation and recall
5	Make it short	Limit it to 2–6 min to maximize concentration and engagement
6	Make it social	Incorporate social media, discussion forums, and polls
7	Make it mobile-friendly	Keep the design simple, clear, and adaptable (Kohnke, 2021)

Embracing microlearning on mobile devices offers numerous benefits, including timely access to content and resources, the consolidation of essential information, and the inclusion of various modalities such as podcasts, infographics, videos, and images (Souza & Amaral, 2014). Microlearning enables students to receive specific information in an engaging and interactive format by presenting key learning objectives simply and clearly. Implementing some of the tips, strategies, and activities outlined in this book can heighten learners' engagement and motivate them. By doing so, you will also help your students improve their English language proficiency.

References

Baumfield, V., Hall, E., & Wall, K. (2013). *Action research in education: Learning through practitioner inquiry.* Sage.

Burns, A., Edwards, E., & Ellis, N. J. (2022). *Sustaining action research: A practical guide for institutional engagement.* Routledge.

Dolasinski, M. J., & Reynolds, J. (2021). Microlearning in the higher education hospitality classroom. *Journal of Hospitality & Tourism Education.* https://doi.org/10.1080/10963758.2021.196 3748

Donahue, M. (2016). Microlearning and the incredible shrinking attention span. *Hotel Management, 231*(7), 27.

Epp, C. D., & Phirangee, K. (2019). Explore mobile tool integration: Design activities carefully or students may not learn. Contemporary *Educational Psychology, 59.* https://doi.org/10.1016/j.cedpsych.2019.101791

Kohnke, L. (2021). Optimizing microlearning for mobile learning. In J. R. Corbeil, M. E. Corbeil, & B. H. Khan (Eds.), *Microlearning in the digital age: The design and delivery of learning in snippets* (pp. 80–94). Routledge.

Lee, Y. M. (2021). Mobile microlearning: A systematic literature review and its implications. *Interactive Learning Environments.* https://doi.org/10.1080/10494820.2021.1977964

McNiff, J., & Whitehead, J. (2011). *All you need to know about action research* (2nd ed.). Sage.

Mohammed, G. S., Wakil, K., & Nawroly, S. S. (2018). The effectiveness of microlearning to improve students' learning ability. *International Journal of Educational Research Review, 3*(3), 32–38. https://doi.org/10.24331/ijere.415824

Souza, M. I., & Amaral, S. F. (2014). Educational microcontent for mobile learning virtual environments. *Creative Education, 5,* 672–681.

Winger, A. (2018). Supersized tips for implementing microlearning in macro ways. *Distance Learning, 15*(4), 51–55.

The manufacturer's authorised representative in the EU is Springer
Nature Customer Service Centre GmbH, Europaplatz 3, 69115 Heidelberg,
Germany. If you have any concerns regarding our products, please
contact ProductSafety@springernature.com

Printed and bound by CPI Group (UK) Ltd, Croydon, CR0 4YY

29/04/2026

02099526-0004